The Black Book:

Reflections From The Baltimore Grassroots

The Black Book:

Reflections From The Baltimore Grassroots

Lawrence Grandpre & Dayvon Love

Leaders of a Beautiful Struggle

2014

First Printing: 2014

ISBN: 978-1-312-51247-4

Leaders of a Beautiful Struggle
231 Holiday Street
Baltimore, MD 21201

www.lbsbaltimore.com

Table of Contents

Introduction

By Dayvon Love

We offer a perspective that is often shut out by mainstream political discussions and by academia, because it questions the very structures that have become essential building blocks for civil society. We are making assertions that many people in mainstream political positions refuse to say, since their employment and consequent ability to move up in the professional world rests on keeping these truths out of the public domain. As grassroots activists, we are committed to building authentic community power, without chasing grants or being in good favor with established institutions. Our stance has made it difficult to sustain the work that we do, but because we hold no allegiances, we are able to say the things that you will read here.

This text is a part of the New Timbuktu Project, a thoroughly independent, alternative learning community of activists, citizen scholars, and professional academics that fosters dialogue centered on the heart of the issues that undermine the livelihoods of Black people. To sustain that community, we channel the wisdom of our ancestors and our elders and apply it to contemporary socio-political issues. Reorienting scholarship from the academy to the lived realities of Black life in America will produce material benefits for Black people. As activists scholars, we see ourselves as functioning within a lineage of Black intellectuals who realized that the division between the "college bubble" and "the real world" is illusory and counterproductive. Instead, this text pulls from our experience doing activist work in the Baltimore community and our academic experiences in the world of intercollegiate policy debate to bring unique perspectives to both activism and academia. To take this discussion further, we invite readers to download New Timbuktu cell phone app, a collection of audio-visual resources created by like-minded scholars and activists, with an online community for New Timbuktu participants and interested citizens.

Though we direct our text to people who have already engaged issues of racism and Black liberation, we are looking beyond an academic audience. Lawrence and I are grassroots activists whose background in collegiate policy debate gave us the skills and intellectual rigor to engage high-level academic material. This has been an integral part to the method and strategy in building Leaders of a Beautiful Struggle.

Lawrence and I are a combination of Afropessimist and Pan-Afrikan nationalist. Afro-Pessimist— an inquiry into Black life predicated on the idea that American civil society is fundamentally organized on the structural positioning of the slave — contends that civil society is fundamentally structured in opposition to Blackness and Black people. Pan-Afrikan nationalism supports global self-determination for people of African descent. I am more of a Pan-Afrikan nationalist than Afro-pessimist and Lawrence is more of a Afro-pessimist than Pan-Afrikan nationalist. This balance grounds our experience in the lives and experiences of Black people. We are carving out a political space where the notion of Black self-determination is not imbued with the baggage loaded onto terms like "black power", predicated on the claim that the development of independent Black institutions is essential for Black liberation. We can no longer rely on white people's benevolence and goodwill to uplift our people. We must build our own power, so that we can engage in the political arena from a position of strength.

Is our focus on Black self-determination too myopic? Some say yes, yet all groups have the right and responsibility to speak on their own behalf. In the public sphere, racial, cultural and ethnic groups advocate for their collective interest. Jewish Americans have organizations nationally like AIPAC and organizations locally like The Associated that speak to their specific issues. Latino Americans have organizations and institutions that are designed specifically to protect and advocate for their interest. Baltimore boasts Casa de Maryland and the Latino Providers Network, both designed specifically to address issues of particular concern to Latino Americans. Public anxiety about the existence of these organizations is largely relegated to right-wing extremists, and such interest groups are not expected asked to address the concerns of other oppressed groups.

Conversely, groups widely associated with dealing with issues facing Black people are uniquely burdened with inclusive agendas reflected in their mission statements. For instance, according to the mission posted on its official website, the NAACP says that it fights for social justice for all Americans. This is an organization that many people think of as being accountable to Black people, but its mission implies otherwise. This is not to pick on the NAACP, but to demonstrate how Black institutions have an unspoken imperative to speak broadly about issues of justice, instead of specifically about our issues. We are allies in the struggle for freedom and liberation for other oppressed groups, but we engage this broader struggle against white supremacy and US imperialism from the position of strict advocacy for independent Black institutions. We speak in this text as Black people who have the right and responsibility to represent ourselves and our own interests.

Much of the engagement with the intellectual ideas in this book happened in the context of competitive policy debate, which in turn birthed Leaders of a Beautiful Struggle (LBS). LBS was founded in 2010 by former policy debaters who are also alumnae of the Baltimore Urban Debate League. Baltimore was one of many cities around the country that started urban debate leagues in order to give students access to policy debate, an argumentation style with very specific conventions and norms distinct from other forms of public speaking. Competitive policy debate has less emphasis on rhetorical skills, and is more focused on developing rigorous, evidence-based argumentation. In Baltimore, we were fortunate enough to come across college debaters and coaches who were challenging the conventions of policy debate, including people like Elizabeth Jones, Daryl Burch, Andy Ellis, David Peterson and many others who came to Baltimore for summer camp during the years that we were entering college debate. Their contributions to policy debate helped to create fertile ground for the immense growth of what would come out of Baltimore, now a hub of people going into college debate and challenging the conventions of competitive policy debate. New innovations in debate included the use of the scholarly works of Black scholars that were previously not used in debate, the incorporation of poetry/hip hop, and the use of performance in the presentation of debate arguments. These innovations were important challenges to the overwhelmingly white male-privileged activity that often perpetuated the invisibility of white supremacy that is so commonplace in our society.

Following the introduction, this text consists of two sections. The first contains the political theories and commentary that guide our work; the second, reflections on the specific work that we have done here in Baltimore, applying some of the ideas in the first section. Both sections flow from the assumption of race literacy on the readers' parts. Also, these essays are our reflections. We are essentially putting our thoughts on paper, so there is no specific academic format for the essays. Each essay was written at different points in time that are reflective of our thoughts about broad political issues.

Many people treat conversations about race differently than they treat other social issues. They make authoritative statements about race but have not engaged in a systematic study of it. Race is relegated to something that anybody can have an opinion on, but does not require any real expertise to discuss intelligently. Our position is that the literacy on issues of race in America is so low that it keeps otherwise smart people from having substantive conversations. For instance, racism and bigotry are not synonymous. Racism is the combination of prejudice and power. Historically, white people's individual bigotry did not create the wretched conditions that oppressed Black people; rather, those people established institutions that wielded material and existential power to operationalize white supremacist ideology over the lives of Black people. Put simply, racism is not about being mean; it is about the power that white people have developed through their exploitation of Black people and other people of color.

Taken a step further, racial justice is not about people being nice to people of other races; it seeks and results in equitable distribution of power so that Black people and others are not reliant on the benevolence of white people in order to ensure our own quality of life. It does not matter if white people hate Black people if we have the institutions to protect ourselves from assaults on our humanity and can maintain our own quality of life. Liking Black people is not racial justice. Relinquishing resources to Black organizations to empower the community is racial justice.

Racism is also commonly understood as describing a person's intentions. We are taught to see racism as character flaw that is only corrected when people stop intentionally being mean and stop hating Black people. This notion oversimplifies racism as centered around bias and bigotry and takes the conversation away from understanding power, the practical effects of a given set of policies or behaviors. One can be complicit in racism without actively engaging in it. Most of us are socialized to internalize racist attitudes and behaviors that seem completely rational. For instance, if I were to say that the financial industry is racist, you might ask me to prove that there is a collective intention to harm Black people by the financial industry. Such a challenge cannot be met. Instead, I would focus on the racial effects that certain policies have. A 2008 study done by the NAACP shows that Black people were more likely to get subprime loans than their white counterparts. This places a financial burden on Black people that has the effect of giving white people greater access to wealth. Houses are a huge source of wealth generation and having less access to home ownership puts us at a severe disadvantage in the marketplace. While I could not point to an individual or group of people who overtly intended to being racist, the financial industry itself has racialized effects that disproportionately hurt Black people. The intention-based definition of racism would exclude the important conversation about Black people having more barriers to wealth development than our white counterparts. Therefore, only an effects-based definition gives us the lens through which we can comprehensively analyze visible inequalities so that we can develop concrete, effective solutions.

Having defined racism, we now look at the contexts in which people invoke "race" where other terms are more accurate. Race is often used interchangeably with ethnicity, nationality and culture, when each term is distinct from the others. For our purposes, race refers to a marker of identity that is based on skin color and other physical characteristics; nationality, a marker of identity shared by people with the same legal relationship to an established state; ethnicity, a people group with a shared history and geography; and culture, the totality of thought and practices that constitutes a lens through which a people group interprets and navigates the world. All four concepts are related but have different meanings and histories. Because race as constructed in America was used by European colonizers to categorize other racial groups as inferior, thereby justifying those groups' oppression, the notion of "not seeing race" is a noble idea. But the idea that one should not see culture is different. We would ask Chinese people to give up their language, cuisine and their customs so that we can all be the same? I don't think so. People have a right to their own cultural traditions, and the celebration of one's own culture does not denigrate anyone else. You can be proud of your culture without putting down someone else's. This is why it is important to be precise about the terms we use when we are discussing issues of race. Imprecisely using aforementioned terms produces misunderstandings that undermine the development of race literacy.

Below are a few general concepts that will be recurring themes throughout the book.

African/Black - There is an ongoing conversation about how people or African descent in America should identify ourselves. Certain scholars and ideological positions place a great deal of importance on whether we call ourselves "Africans" or "Black." Those who insist on using "African" often do so to emphasize the importance of our African heritage as the starting point and framework for interpreting our existence in America. Critics of that viewpoint say that it romanticizes African culture and obscures the culture we have produced here in the US. Those who insist calling ourselves "Black" do so to stress that the Middle Passage stripped us of our African culture and resulted in the creation of a different culture. In this text, we will use both terms interchangeably. We will argue that Black people in the US should relate to ancient Africa the same way that Europeans relate to ancient Greece. We have a distinct culture here as Black people, but we are a part of the larger African diaspora that shares a historical legacy.

African-Centered - Denotes a broad field of scholarship that emphasizes the intellectual and cultural resources found in the study of ancient African civilizations. This is a paradigm that is not often represented in mainstream academic conversations, but is a core component of our intellectual framework for this book.

Anti-Blackness - Describes the political system which has been produced via the global tendency to associate Blackness with negative characteristics, and specifically within the American outlook on Blackness as a "zero-point" of slavery and negativity. We pull from the work of Frank Wilderson, who argues that, since the Arab slave trade during the 11th century, a global system has emerged to define Black/African people as subhuman, continuing through today to produce racial disparities unique to the Black community.

Black Nationalism/Pan-African Nationalism - Used interchangeably to refer to the idea that Black people should control the economic, political, and social institutions in our communities.

Racism/White Supremacy - Extends beyond known hate groups like the Ku Klux Klan to encompass the social, political and economic domination of people of color by white people. This text will substantiate the claim that we live in a society founded on white supremacy, closely related to anti-blackness, which some scholars prefer over white supremacy because it more precisely describes the nature of white supremacy. We draw from scholars like Neely Fuller Jr. and Dr. Francis Cress Welsing in using white supremacy, which already assumes the anti-blackness as the inherent logic of white supremacy.

Section One

Anti-Blackness as (Independent) Political System

One analogy which can be applied to the work of interrogating racism is peeling an onion: the more you work, the more layers you find in need of stripping.

And the more you may find yourself crying.

In line with this, it may be somewhat frustrating for many who have begun to develop an understanding of racism that in addition to challenging implicit racial bias, questioning the sufficiency of multiculturalism, and grappling with the notion of white supremacy as a political system, that there is an entire layer of racial analysis yet to be peeled. Indeed, while it may seem a logical corollary to a general understanding of racism, understanding anti-Blackness as an independent political system, mutually constitutive with but separate from capitalism, is an essential step toward understanding and disrupting the complex mechanics of American racism.

The Myth of "Comprehensive" Class First Analysis

While color-blindness remains a dominant discourse in many corporate and mainstream conversations, discussion among progressives and liberals is often dominated by the notion that it is economic inequality and poverty, not racism, which is the major problem. These discussions usually operate under the popular definition of racism as individual bias against a particular racial group. While individual racial bias has indeed become less overt (but far from nonexistent), these discussions too often focus almost exclusively on the individual level, obscuring the continuing prevalence of racism, and in this case specifically anti-Blackness, as a political and social system. An understanding of anti-Blackness reveals the "class first" argument to be myopic, as there are several examples of disparate outcomes between Blacks and Whites that cannot be explained through the framework of class.

Examples of anti-Blackness as an independent political system can be seen at nearly every level of American society. Even when controlling for class, Blacks are more likely to be exposed to environmental hazards like highways, trash incinerators, and power plants, a sign of "environmental racism" (Ballard, 2000). This environmental racism has been linked to higher rates of exposure to environmental toxins, which has been used to explain why Blacks have higher rates of asthma across class lines (ibid). Blacks regardless of class get lower quality health care and suffer worse health outcomes, outcomes generally linked to less access to quality care even among affluent Blacks, but which can in many instances be linked to anti-Black bias in the health care system. Controlling for class, Blacks get less pain medication than Whites for similar aliments, as well as ½ as many recommendations for potentially lifesaving heart surgeries (Hoberman, 2012). Black women were also more likely to receive hysterectomies than White women suffering from similar ailments. In housing, Blacks receive 18% less when selling their homes than Whites with similar houses in similar neighborhoods, which combined with Blacks being 5-8 times more likely to be targeted by subprime lenders led to Blacks nationwide losing 50% of their wealth in the great recession (Hoerlyck, 2003, Wicks-Lim, 2012). This is on top of the numerous studies done that show prospective Black renters, even with similar employment and credit status with whites, are denied housing 10 to 15 percent more often, sometimes only for "sounding" Black on a phone interview or having a "Black sounding" name (Demby, 2013). The presence of verifiable racial inequities even when controlling for class as a variable shows the notion of "compressive" class analysis as more convenient fiction than empirical fact, at least in relation to Blacks in America.

The most jarring examples of anti-Black bias can be seen in the criminal justice system. While Blacks make up 12% of America's population, they make up almost 40% of America's prison population, a fact that can only be understood as an extension of policing tactics established in the Jim Crow south (Alexander, 2010). In the specific instance of marijuana arrests, despite equal rates of marijuana use among Whites and Blacks, Blacks were nationwide 3.73 times more likely to be arrested than Whites for marijuana possession (ACLU, 2013). These disparities could not be explained by geography, personal bias, or class, but only through the selective enforcement of drug laws to target Black and Brown citizens (ibid). In Baltimore, Blacks were a staggering 5.6 times more likely than Whites to be arrested for marijuana possession, the highest disparity in Maryland. These racial disparities continue once in the criminal justice system, with Blacks in Baltimore almost 3 times less likely than Whites statewide to have their cases resolved at intake or through informal means, meaning Blacks were 3 times more likely to face jail for similar crimes than Whites, who are more often given community service and fines as punishment (Open Society Institute, 2011). Some states treat substance abuse by pregnant women on welfare as a criminal offense (assault on the unborn child), yet it is poor Black women who are far more likely than poor Whites to be prosecuted under these laws, and more likely to be forced by court order to undergo cesareans and have the babies turned over to the state (Palthrow and Flavin, 2012). The disparities extend to the most extreme forms of state violence, with states putting Blacks to death via capital punishment at a rate 40% higher than Whites for comparable crimes (Dieter, 1998). The final statistic shows what's at stake in this analysis. Supplementing class first analysis with an understanding of anti-Blackness is not just a matter of being politically correct, it is, in the most extreme example of capital punishment, literally a matter of life and death, and as such requires serious attention from scholars and activists.

The Legacy of Slavery: Anti-Blackness as Political System

William Faulkner once wrote "The past is never dead. It's not even past", illuminating how despite attempts to categorize historical events as irrelevant to the present, they have a tendency to continually manifest themselves. This is a good starting point to understand how past policies and biases have created the contemporary political system of anti-Blackness. The above statistics only make sense within the context of a national history of anti-Black thinking and anti-Black policymaking, a history that once understood makes the functions of anti-Blackness visible.

A discussion of medical anti-Blackness can be instructive in understating how the contemporary system of anti-Blackness is linked to slavery. University of Texas-Austin professor John Hoberman links the disparate treatment of Black and White patients to the medicalization of stereotypes that have their roots in slavery. He details racial thinking in various seemingly colorblind and objective judgments made by doctors. For example, Hoberman sought to understand the racial disparity in pain medication prescriptions. He observed that many doctors seemed to treat Blacks as having a higher pain threshold than Whites, but also showed less trust in Black patients to adhere to medication use recommendations (a higher fear of "noncompliance" with doctors' orders) (Hoberman). Both these notions can be traced to stereotypes born in slavery, where the mythology of the strong Black body justified putting slaves to work, and the myth of the irrational Black mind justified denying certain freedoms and rights (i.e. fear that intoxicated slaves would become violent or become "noncompliant") (ibid). He applies this thinking to explain other disparities. High blood pressure is more likely to be seen as "normal" for Blacks considering what many doctors perceive as their innately volatile emotional dispositions, explaining the decreased recommendations for heart surgery (ibid). Also, Black women with symptoms of endometriosis (severe menstual cramps) were more likely to be misdiagnosed as having pelvic inflammatory disease (a common symptom of venereal disease), a fact Hoberman links to the myth founded in slavery of Black female hyper sexuality (ibid). This myth of hyper sexuality could explain the higher rates of Black female hysterectomies, with doctors believing they are doing black women a favor by preventing unplanned pregnancies.

Hoberman shows these links in a specific context, one that is essential for a proper analysis of anti-Blackness. Nowhere does he explain these actions as those of individual, racist doctors, but he explains how these ideas have become the definition of "good medicine" which well-meaning, even ostensibly progressive medical professionals are adopting. This demonstrates how anti-Blackness is not a question of individual bias, but a pervasive system embedded in social institutions.

An analysis of what happens when anti-Black thinking is brought to a macro/policy level gives a framework for understanding how anti-Blackness perpetuates itself. Hoberman gives the following example:

"...in February 1992 when Dr. Frederick K. Goodwin, then administrator of the Alcohol, Drug Abuse, and Mental Health Administration, commented on the so-called Violence Initiative ...According to Goodwin's evolutionary model, the male violence of the black American ghetto was a reversion to the chaos of the primeval African jungle and its primitive inhabitants. Male monkeys, he said, are violent and hypersexual, suggesting 'some interesting evolutionary implications.' The progeny produced by their frequent copulations will 'offset the fact that half of them are dying.' He then proposed an analogy with 'inner city areas' and 'the loss of some of the civilizing evolutionary things that we have built up. . . . Maybe it isn't just the careless use of the word when people call certain areas of certain cities, jungles.'... The medical and social implications of the Violence Initiative were clear. As the African American political scientist Ronald Walters put it: 'If there is a reason for this kind of research, the aim is to find a drug. And if you begin using drugs to pacify young black males, as is often done with Ritalin for hyperactivity, you're creating a regime of social control.' " (ibid).

Here separate social institutions begin to weave together to unveil the larger structure of anti- Blackness. History and anthropology create notions of dangerous Blacks, which get carried into the medical profession and educational training. Once Black children reach school, teachers educated within an academic curriculum laden with tacit and overt anti-Blackness see normal childhood behavior as degenerate. This creates an environment where Black kids are not likely to be seen as evolving youth, but instead as problems needing to be "solved", first through medical interventions, as shown by the higher rates of ADHD diagnosis for elementary age Black children, then criminalization, shown by higher rates of suspensions, expulsions, and arrests for middle/high school aged Black students (NAACP, 2005). Once criminalized, a judge then is more likely to see Black youth as needing punitive measures due to the long standing notion of innate Black criminality, creating increased rates of Black youth incarceration. Once released, without access to job training, college grants (denied to felons) or even the right to vote in many states, a sense of forced helplessness leads many to illegal survival tactics which drives recidivism and thus provides more "proof" of Black deviance, fueling the academic/anthropological assumptions that started the cycle in the first place. The ACLU is correct to see this as a "school to prison pipeline", but it is necessary to see how anti- Blackness provides much of foundational logic (the "pressure" within the pipeline analogy) that keeps this pipeline moving.

At every level, the teacher who mistakes childhood play for a budding deviance, the doctor who sees a pathology in need of medication and not an individual in need of therapy, and the judge who sees a future career criminal in need of deterrence and not a youth in need of rehabilitation, individual judgments meld with institutional power, which forms anti-Black bias into a political system of anti-Blackness. It's also important to note that, as anti-Blackness is about systemic power and not individual bias, having Black and Brown people in positions of authority does not preclude them from serving the functions of the system of anti-Blackness, especially as many minorities are forced to internalize the systems logic as a means of professional survival and advancement. That the official in Hoberman's example entered the government as a Regan appointee but later was promoted by Clinton to head of the National Institute of Mental Health shows how this system spans the political and ideological spectrum, a fact that must be taken into account when attempting to theorize and undermine anti-Blackness.

Theory in Action: "Obamacare" as Case-Study in Anti-Blackness

Anti-Blackness is an essential heuristic for understanding contemporary politics. The Affordable Care Act (also known as the "ACA" but popularly known as "Obamacare") provides a good case study in how anti-

8

Blackness has national political implications, and an analysis of how anti-Blackness functions in this instance shows how theorizations using this framework provide necessary insights which dominant liberal/progressive discourses overlook.

Despite being traditionally seen within the context of capitalism, the neoliberal political framework which has been used to attack the ACA, with its focus on privatization and smaller government, must be seen also as an extension of anti-Blackness. University of California–Irvine professor David Goldberg explains the racial history behind neoliberal resistance to the welfare state, writing:

> "...racial meanings have animated neoliberal attacks on the welfare state...attacks on affirmative action reveal a deeper critical concern for neoliberals troubled over race. In the U.S., neoconservative critics of the state implicitly identify it as representing blackness and the interests thought most directly to advance black life. As a result both of serious application of antidiscrimination legislation and of affirmative action policies, the state became the single largest employer of African Americans. The perception among critics of these programs accordingly devolved into the view that black people are either employed as beneficiaries of affirmative action or they are supported by welfare. In short, from the 1970s on, the state increasingly came to be conceived as a set of institutions supporting the undeserving (recall the identification of Bill Clinton as 'the first black President,' first by Toni Morrison but taken up quickly by neoconservatives out to do him in). Fear of a black state is linked to worries about a black

planet, of alien invasion and alienation, of a loss of local and global control and privilege long associated with whiteness. Neoliberalism, therefore, can be read as a response to this concern about the impending impotence of whiteness. " (Goldberg, 2007).

Written under the Bush administration, this "fear of a black state" Goldberg postulates must be magnified exponentially under the Obama presidency. Thus, one of Obama's central political failings was thinking the major political force nationwide to be a generic "citizenry" who, while concerned with personal freedom and government intrusion, can be persuaded by reason and economic benefits. In many states, however, the dominant force is the political system of anti-Blackness, a system which produces a white racialized polity whose fear of being controlled by a racial other operates outside the realm of rational political and even economic persuasion.

This anti-Blackness can be seen by investigating specific political outcomes related to the ACA. The administration was blindsided by two unforeseen developments in its Obamacare roll out. First, many conservative governors and legislatures rejected federal funds for an ACA proposed expansion of Medicare. Second, many of these states also refused to run their own online health insurance exchanges, leaving the Federal government forced to step in and run them. The Obama administration operated under the assumption that even recalcitrant states would not turn down free money, and that their sense of states' rights would push them to run their own exchanges rather than have the Federal government run an exchange for them.

What the administration failed to account for was how anti-Blackness changes the political equation for red state governors and legislators. Using Goldberg's analysis, Obamacare symbolically represents the contemporary "impotence of whiteness" meaning full scale public rejection of the law allows the politicians in these state to embody a "virile" white identity, protecting the citizenry from Obamacare and the symbolic threat of being controlled by Blackness it carries with it. This mirrors Northwestern University professor Charles Mills' analysis on the political implications of what W.E.B. DuBois called "the wages of whiteness". He postulated that even in instances where it is materially beneficial for Whites to align with Blacks (i.e. states getting free Federal money to run the health care exchanges and expand Medicare), the psychological attachment to whiteness would be seen as more valuable, and red state resistance to ACA provides empirical validation of this theory (Mills, 2004).

Anti- Blackness is also essential to understanding another concept which drives the rejection of Medicare dollars. With the prominent social legacy of the "Welfare Queen", beneficiaries of state programs for the poor have been racially "blackened", a move that allows them to be defined as outside the political community and therefore making an illegitimate claim for state help. Thus, despite that fact that most welfare and Medicare recipients nationwide are White, and in many of these specific states most of the benefits would go to poor, white, GOP voters, the constituents and the politicians saw the psychological capital of embodying the white ideal as more valuable than the material benefits given by what was seen as "tainted" money (Quadango, 1994).

Democrats and progressives often wonder why poor white Republicans vote "against their self-interests." An understanding of anti-Blackness reveals these votes are actually not against their self-interest, as the dominant progressive/liberal framework fails to see that these interests are not just economic, but largely, sometimes even predominantly, racial.

Conclusion: The Need for a New Paradigm

From local to national politics, anti-Blackness is a system of coding the world and rendering it coherent, one that must be accounted for when creating political solutions. Michelle Alexander gives an example of this when she rejects color blind solutions to mass incarcerations, saying that without an analysis of the Drug War as a racial caste system, even political moves to dismantle the policy framework of the Drug War would fail to disrupt the *racial* framework of society (Alexander, 2010). To summarize her argument, it is a fundamental misunderstanding to see the Drug War as a *failed* attempt at drug control policymaking; one must see the Drug War as a *successful* attempt at racialized social control via imprisonment. Dismantling these specific laws thus fails to eliminate the dangerous nexus of racial fear that produced the current system and would produce another system should the current system be disrupted.

A tangible application of this insight would be to question the value of recently proposed libertarian/ progressive coalitions on drug legalization and drug policy.

While this coalition might agree on ending drug prohibitions, adopting the libertarian individual rights framework would risk bolstering the notions of "personal responsibility", which in an anti-Black society, are loaded concepts. The same logic of "individual freedom" that the coalition might strategically adopt to advance the decriminalization agenda would be turned against essential parts of a comprehensive justice agenda, like publicly funded drug rehabilitation programs and reparations for (predominantly Black) communities decimated by the War on Drugs.

This practical policy example shows the necessity for a new political framework that evaluates anti-Blackness as central to the formation of contemporary politics, with the hope that by asking better questions, activists and scholars can begin to find better answers to the problems which plague America today.

Work Cited

ACLU Foundation. *The War on Marijuana in Black and White*. Rep. American Civil Liberties Union, June 2013. Web. 17 Nov. 2013.

Alexander, Michelle. *The New Jim Crow: Mass Incarceration in the Age of Colorblindness*. New York: New, 2010. Print.

Arifuku, Isami, Antoinette Davis, and Monique Morris. *WHY ARE SO MANY AFRICAN AMERICAN YOUTH ENTANGLED IN BALTIMORE CITY'S JUSTICE*

SYSTEM: AN EXPLORATION. Rep. Baltimore: Open Society Institute, 2011. Print.

Bullard, Robert D. *Dumping in Dixie: Race, Class, and Environmental Quality*. Boulder, Colo: Westview, 2000. Print.

Demby, Gene. *For People Of Color, A Housing Market Partially Hidden From View.* Code Switch. National Public. 17 June 2013. Web. 18 Nov. 2013

Dieter, Richard. *The Death Penalty in Black and White: Who Lives, Who Dies, Who Decides*. Rep. Death Penalty Information Center, June 1998. Web. 17 Nov. 2013

Goldberg, David T. (2007) *"Neoliberalizing Race,"* Macalester Civic Forum: Vol. 1: Iss. 1, Article 14. Web. 17 Nov. 2013

Hoerlyck, Anders. "Racial Disparity Still Haunts Housing Market." *Johns Hopkins Institute for Policy Studies*. Johns Hopkins University, 03 July 2003. Web. 17 Nov. 2013.

Mills, Charles. "Racial Exploitation and the Wages of Whiteness." *What White Looks Like: African-American Philosophers on the Whiteness Question*. Ed. George Yancy. New York: Routledge, 2004. N. page. Print.

NAACP Legal defense and Educational Fund. *Dismantling the School-to-prison Pipeline*. Rep. New York, NY: National Association for the Advancement of Colored People, 2005. Web. 17 Nov. 2013

Paltrow, Lynn, and Jeanne Flavin. "Arrests of and Forced Interventions on Pregnant Women in the United States, 1973-2005: Implications for Women's Legal Status and Public Health." *Journal of Health Politics, Policy & Law* 38.299 (2013): n. pag.*Racism.org*. Web. 17 Nov. 2013.

Quadagno, Jill S. *The Color of Welfare: How Racism Undermined the War on Poverty*. New York: Oxford UP, 1996. Print.

Wicks-Lim, Jeannette. "The Great Recession in Black Wealth White Wealth Reaches Historic High of Twenty times Black Wealth." *Political Economy Research Institute*. University of Massachusetts Amherst, 19 Jan. 2012. Web. 17 Nov. 2013.

Pan Afrikan Nationalism Defined

By Dayvon Love

The term "Pan-Afrikan nationalism" is used interchangeably with "Black nationalism" to honor and respect Dr. John Henrik Clarke and Mama Marimba Ani, Dr. Clarke's student and (an) elder. This essay is written under the spiritual and intellectual guidance of these two giants in the Black liberation struggle.

The central issue that faces people of African descent is the development of socially, economically and politically independent Black institutions. Any conversation that does not substantiate this claim plays into the interests of established, White political power, built upon 246 years of chattel slavery. Though many Black activists engage the left as natural political allies, both sides of the mainstream, left-right discourse are devoted to sustaining the generational wealth that Whites have accumulated through free labor, withheld resources and obstructed access. As Dr. John Henrik Clarke once said, "the left and the right have us wrong." The political right promotes cutting government spending on social programs that barely alleviate historical disparities on the premise that the beneficiaries are primarily Black and therefore undeserving, embodied by caricatures like the welfare queen. Conversely, the left advocates for increased spending on social programs in order to finance White-operated and controlled nonprofits. Either way, White interests remain the focus.

Consider how left-right politics is framed in mainstream discourse. The left stands for racial integration, a key indicator and goal of "progress"; the right, homogeneity without government intervention, i.e. segregation. This model rarely takes into account whether integration was effective for improving the collective quality of life of Black people. Many luminaries of the Civil Rights Movement said no, it does not. Malcolm X often remarked about lunacy of integration, arguing that the idea of asking White people to accept us into their institutions requires that we depend on White benevolence. He argued that we are better off creating and carrying out our own solutions than looking to oppressors for liberation. He drew the only logical conclusion, given the record that White supremacist institutions had with addressing Black people's concerns. In his debate with Bayard Rustin, Malcolm X argued that segregation refers to second-class citizenship, but separation means having independent institutions of equal caliber to those of Whites. However, the notion of having separate Black institutions is often represented as being motivated by hate, as opposed to what Malcolm X observed as mere common sense.

With regard to public, K-12 education, integration has yielded poor results. White families resisted forced legal integration en masse, "fleeing" the cities to live in federally subsidized suburbs and taking with them the substantial tax base that funds quality school districts. Gutted of essential resources, schools have deployed incomplete solutions, like recruiting middle-class White teachers into predominantly working-class and impoverished Black communities, where those teachers naively expect that they can educate Black youth without having immersed themselves in the history and culture of Black people. There are isolated incidences of success in charter schools, like the Harlem Children's Zone, but they require tremendous resources to produce their outcomes.

Amos Wilson once said that the purpose of education is to "train its students to protect and perpetuate the national interest." This means that students should be trained in the skills and knowledge necessary to improve their communities. Currently, our education system teaches young people how to be objects in the larger, American body politic, instead of agents and producers of their own political and economic institutions.

Teaching entrepreneurship and vocational skills like plumbing, electrical work, and other building trades are excluded from the conversation about educating Black children in favor of producing loyal, liberal democratic subjects, yet these skills are vital for build an indigenous economic base from which independent institutions can grow and flourish. In other words, if we live in a society based on White supremacy and anti-blackness, then as people of African descent, we have different material interests than our White counterparts, and we need an education model that reflects that. Promoting integration as racial justice inhibits Black self-determination.

Mainstream media describes our challenge to White supremacy merely as resentment. Journalist Mike Wallace famously hosted a documentary in 1959 on the Nation of Islam called "The Hate That Produced Hate", which described Elijah Muhammad's objectives as being rooted in hatred of White people. In fact, the Nation of Islam espouses Black self-reliance, under the assumption that, since America has failed to deal justly with Black people, we should separate and do for ourselves. In fact, the Nation's ethos strongly parallels the impetus for the Boston Tea Party and the Declaration of Independence, borne out of British colonists' resistance to monarchical tyranny. When oppressed people poise themselves for revolution, they do not concern themselves with the emotional perceptions of the oppressor class; they act decisively to regain their own social, economic and political autonomy.

For integration to reverse centuries of Black oppression, it would need majority White support, historically in woefully short supply. Jim Lowen in his book Sundown Towns says that 85% of White people live in communities that are either exclusively or predominately populated by other White people. In fact, not until 2003 did the first Black family move into former president George W. Bush's Highland Park neighborhood. President Lyndon B. Johnson's Kerner Commission found that the general collective economic condition of Black people was worse in 1988 than in 1968. Moreover, the Black elite, originally confined to living in and supporting all-Black communities, used to legal desegregation to relocate to formerly restricted, White neighborhoods. Both circumstances decimated Black institutions by reallocating our dollars to pad the wealth of White people. Empirically observed, integration has actually decreased the quality of life for Black people.

During segregation, Black people practiced economic autonomy out of necessity, with considerable success. We controlled how we educated students, our entertainment and social networks. In Baltimore, North Avenue had a vibrant Black nightlife that cultivated indigenous, Black performing artists. Today, many of those establishments have closed their doors or barely meet expenses, and we patronize largely White-owned and operated venues. Much of our political and economic power was rooted in the "base communities" and "vernacular institutions"—indigenous, grassroots, community-based and integral to Black survival during segregation.   Howard McDougall in his book <u>Black Baltimore</u> expands on these concepts as follows:

> "In Baltimore, as we have seen, black participation in both government and the economy was facilitated by the strength of black vernacular culture. Yet an increased role for government in the lives of all Americans, especially after the New Deal, tended to disrupt the vernacular community partly because government took over functions people had once performed themselves, but also because government was used as a tool to create White and black settlements in which community was attenuated. The more upwardly mobile members of the black community resented their confinement in poor, inner-city communities and strove to break out."

Integration did considerable damage to our ability produce and maintain a political and economic power base.

Even Dr. Martin Luther King, Jr., began to question the goal of integration. Harry Belafonte often recalls a conversation that he had with Dr. King five days before his assassination where Dr. King says that he fears that he has integrated his people into a burning house. He concluded that the U.S. had lost its moral conscious in its willingness to invest billions of dollars into fighting the Vietnam war instead of domestic anti-poverty programs. In his essay "Trumpet of Consciousness," Dr. King observed that America needs a "radical redistribution of political power and wealth", contradicting the narrative of Black political inclusion into the American mainstream popularly associated with Dr. King's legacy.

In our continuing struggle for autonomy, Black people draw upon the intellectual and cultural resources of the entire African diaspora, hence the term "Pan-Afrikan nationalism". This term conceptually unites the culture and contributions of Black people in the U.S. with those in the Caribbean and Latin America, and with Black people globally. Unity insulates us from being co-opted into White ideas about our oppression. When scholars not of African descent explain our condition, their widely accepted views subliminally cause us to believe that we can best articulate our views through White interpreters.

Karl Marx's work is often used in the academy to explain Black oppression. However, Marx developed his theories amidst London and urban centers in Germany, neither notably populated by people of African descent. Observations made in one setting—in this case, urban, western Europe—and then universalized to unrelated contexts drown out the voices of people with comprehensive, lived experience. For instance, Marx famously critiqued religion as "the opiate of the poor," a distraction from the injustices perpetrated by the state. Now, in Europe, where the church has historically been a primary state actor, sanctioning and purveying oppression, Marx's assessment may apply. This is not the case for Black people, for whom the church functioned as the first independent Black institution in the Americas, the only one that White people allowed Black people to have. The church was a school, meeting space, hospital, and many other roles that Black people needed in the absence of the formal mechanisms that would normally provide these services. Many Black people were inspired by their revolutionary practice of Christianity to challenge White supremacy, among them Richard Allen, Nat Turner,

Denmark Vessey, David Walker and Sojourner Truth. Applying Marx to this history would discount the revolutionary contributions of the Black church in its fight against oppression. Having neither studied nor based his writings on the African diaspora, Marx cannot accurately be applied to circumstances that are a direct result of White colonialism and the trans-Atlantic slave trade.

The mainstream left challenges all forms of caste systems. While Marx theorized that the European proletariat and bourgeoisie was historically and scientifically determined to clash, Cheikh Anta Diop describes ancient African civilizations with caste systems that had intrinsic, political safeguards to protect the rights and humanity of those in the lower castes. Marx would have us view all caste systems as inherently oppressive to the lower castes. Scholarship presented from an African Centered framework teaches us that Marx and similar thinkers are inadequate to the task of interpreting the Black historical and contemporary condition. They have useful insights, but we must use our scholars and intellectuals to narrate our history and struggle for freedom.

Thusly, we advance Pan-Afrikan nationalism in order to improve the quality of life for people of African descent. In a world based on White supremacy and structured according to anti-blackness, we must have a collective set of institutional structures tasked with empowering Black people specifically. This decisive challenge to White supremacy has been cast as outmoded, essentialist, sexist and homophobic. In an academic space dominated by the White left and with Black people's bodies as specimens and fetish objects, Pan-Afrikan nationalism threatens to remove Black people from the cultural paradigm of European thought and into our indigenous theories and practices. We are heavily incentivized to participate in this circus, with affirmation, money and prestige for doing our work within their boundaries. Indeed, scholars and advocates that root their work in Pan-Afrikan nationalist objectives do not command the same reverence as accepted members of the academic canon. Amos Wilson, Marimba Ani, Dr. John Henrik Clarke, Cheikh Anta Diop, Francis Cress Welsing, Clenoria Weems-Hudson and Nah Dove have produced brilliant scholarship to guide us on how to produce a new world that would affirm our existence. Their work so threatens the White, liberal, academic establishment that it is often erased from conversations about challenging White supremacy.

To be a Pan-Afrikan nationalist is to work toward creating institutional spaces that will protect Black people from White supremacy. It is a worldview, not an exclusive club. Many scholars and activists have used the call for Black power and Pan-Afrikanism to fortify their own personality cults. Dr. John Henrik Clarke once said that one of the biggest effects that White supremacy has had on Black people is the presence of ego starvation. We have been so bombarded with negative images of Black people —as nothing, ugly, stupid, worthless—that we have an existential investment in boosting our self-concept around leading movements instead of advancing principles. Wearing red, black, and green accessories while spouting macho slogans does not further Pan-Afrikan nationalism at the grassroots level, neither does getting sucked into the intellectual rabbit hole of the academy. In <u>Black Africa: The Economic and Cultural Basis for a Federated State</u>, Cheikh Anta Diop describes the intellectual left's impotence at addressing the problems facing Black people:

"Our ideologists have not succeeded in moving revolutionary theory forward by one step in Black Africa. Indeed, though one be armed with so fecund a scientific method of analysis as Marxist dialectics (assuming it had been sufficiently assimilated), it would be hopeless to try to apply it to a reality of which one is totally ignorant. For a long time many of our compatriots have thought they could get by without any deep knowledge of African society and Africa in all aspects: history, language, ethnicities, energy potential, raw materials, and the like. The conclusions reached have often been abysmally banal, when not plain and simply wrong. They have thought they could make up for the lack of ideas, breadth, and revolutionary perspectives by the use of offensive, excessive, and murky vocabulary; they forgot that the truly revolutionary quality of language is its demonstrative clarity based on the objective use of facts and their dialectical relationships, which results in irresistibly convincing the intelligent reader".

Through his insight, Diop implies that we must form concrete solutions to Black oppression, most importantly, through what Clarke calls "nation management." Black people must perfect the practical and business skills needed to build and maintain the infrastructure of a healthy community. At present, we continue to allow our issues to finance the lives and thought experiments of White people, who control both the grantors and grantees. Nation management suggests that we put our emphasis on developing the skills to manage our own institutions and demand the resources to finance them.

Three pioneers of nation management during the early 20th century have gone understated in mainstream political discourse: Booker T. Washington, Marcus Garvey, and Elijah Muhammad. Washington emphasized self-reliance, advocating to provide Black people with basic skills to financially manage our own affairs, yet he is most remembered for his famous dispute with W.E.B. DuBois, often framed as a zero-sum choice between whether Black people should pursue DuBois's aim of political equality or focus on Washington's call for self-sufficiency and delay aspirations for political inclusion. While Washington's unwillingness to address political inequality is cause for concern, the essence of his message was nation management: self-reliance as a prerequisite to establishing political power. DuBois eventually reached the same conclusion in his essay "Education and Work", written after Washington's death. He revisits his key points of contention with Washington, stating:

> "In the case of the industrial school, the practical object was absolutely right, and still is right: that is, the desire of placing in American life a trained black man who could earn a decent living and make that living the foundation stone of his own culture and of the civilization of his group."

In other words, DuBois, too, came to see that Black people cannot have effective political power without a strong economic and social base. Under Washington's leadership, the Tuskegee Institute trained Black people in vocational skills (shoemaking, brick masonry, etc.) that would allow us to be economically self-sufficient. Because self-reliance and self-sufficiency are necessary to attaining Black liberation, Washington's absence from the the left's narration of important Black political ideas exposes White liberals' lack of   interest in authentic Black self-determination. To omit Washington is to reject nation management, which lie at the heart of Pan-Afrikan nationalism.

Marcus Garvey's version of nation management, a potent blend of race/racial pride and entrepreneurship, models how we should develop independent Black institutions. Garvey founded the United Negro Improvement Association (UNIA), which managed the Black Star Steamship Line, a fleet of ships that the UNIA bought to promote commercial cooperation between people of African descent around the world. UNIA also ran a nursing service, the UNIA Black Cross Nurses, which provided vital medical services like first aid, nutritional counseling, and infant healthcare to Black people denied treatment at segregated hospitals. UNIA's voice became the "Negro World", a newspaper that gave a platform to such luminaries as author and anthropologist Zora Neale Hurston, whose work was not as broadly respected as it came to be decades after her death. These kinds of initiatives reflect effective nation management. Current discussions of Garvey's work often reduce it to the "Back to Africa" movement. While Garvey certainly centered Africa in his work, the numerous programs he advanced through UNIA form the true substance of his Pan-Afrikan nationalism.

Though he originated the Nation of Islam, Elijah Muhammad is often disregarded as a significant leader because of his rift with Malcolm X and the children that he fathered with his secretaries. However, his personal rifts and misdeeds do not erase how his methodology advanced Pan-Afrikan nationalism. The Nation's belief that the Black man is the original man—and embodied in God himself—

instilled self-respect among its adherents, counteracting the psychological devastation that Black people endured in a White supremacist society. While mainstream media depict Muhammad's proclamation that White people are inherently devilish as disturbing, this assertion anchors his methodology because it explains the havoc that White people had wrought on Black people and the darker peoples of the world. Black people had been so blinded by White images of God that many of us could not see what White people had done to Black people as criminal. Unleashing dogs, lynching, brutalizing Black protesters, and protecting the perpetrators of those atrocities more than qualifies as devilish behavior. We needed a Black divinity to give us the confidence and imperative to create our own institutions.

Regardless of the split between Elijah Muhammad and Malcolm X, it is important to understand that the program of Elijah Muhammad was essential for unleashing the inherent genius of Malcolm X. The Nation of Islam has produced retail stores, bakeries, schools, and other institutions that instilled a sense of Black nationhood into the communities they serve. Malcolm X's departure from the Nation of Islam does not remove his own allegiance to Pan-Afrikan nationalism. His trip to Mecca, and subsequent name change to El-Hajj Malik El-Shabazz, globalizes his philosophical scope while leaving its core intact. When Malcolm X forms the Organization of Afro-American Unity (OAAU), he says that Black nationalism remains his political philosophy and that White people can support the OAAU externally, not as members. Malcolm X does develop an international perspective on addressing U.S. imperialism, but through a Pan Afrikan nationalist lens. This reading of his post-Nation activism contradicts how some radicals use his critique of capitalism to frame him as a leader seeking to transcend—thus erase—his Blackness, dissolving into a universal struggle against capitalism. Yet he remains resolutely, unambiguously, and advocate of Black self determination.

To be sure, Washington, Garvey, and Muhammad each have problematic aspects to their legacies that warrant intensive criticism, but the dedication to nation management the core of their work is essential to Black empowerment.

Pan-Afrikan nationalism in the academy

People of African descent have a particular material and existential relationship to the world that requires a distinct set of intellectual tools for properly navigating this White supremacist society. One of the most devastating elements of Europe's global domination has been how it has projected its own epistemology as the universal lens from which all people have been taught to interpret the world. Even how we conceive and interpret ideas has been colonized, prompting us to divorce from the minds that generate them. For instance, if a Black person were to say, "I hate White people," this would be popularly heard as hate speech and rebutted with the argument, "What if a White person said they hate Black people? That would be racist, right? So it's the same thing if a Black person says they hate White people." Such an exchange demonstrates the European cultural belief in disembodied ideas. This response only makes sense if the bodies and the experiences of the people making these statements are disconnected from the ideas themselves. Black people have endured immeasurable violence at the hands of White people over the past four centuries. An expression of hatred from the survivors toward to the perpetrators that grows out of historical memory and current experiences, while sad, does not credibly equate with the reinforcement of existing oppression. Categorizing ideas as abstractions reflects the European cultural ethos. An African cultural paradigm understands that the same ideas and words mean different things when they are produced from different bodies.

Scholarly critiques of Pan-Afrikan nationalism routinely detach the body from the idea, an outlook George Yancy calls "a view from nowhere." When ideas take on meaning independent of the bodies that birth them, the theorists are not implicated in the actions that flow from those ideas. Decartes, a seminal European philosopher, declares, "I think, therefore I am," disavowing the role of the body in the production of knowledge, casting the body aside as a contaminant that impedes the path to truth. Today, white liberals might say that class should be the primary consideration for understanding the structures of society, without interrogating how this claim impacts their ability to wield power and influence in radical movements. The White, working-class struggle then becomes the universal perspective of all working-class people, allowing White people to take the lead on issues and in settings that affect predominately Black communities. White people's tendency to disconnect the abstract and corporeal supports the status quo, disallowing a set of embodied experiences and structures that require unique approaches to respect the different set of collective embodied experiences.

To unite body and idea, Black people must ground ourselves in a history rooted in our bodies. As people of African descent, we insist on a world that affirms our collective existence, in all spaces and at all times. To recenter our worldview in a Pan-Afrikan nationalist frame, we must first learn to affirm our bodies, to place them in a historical context. Marimba Ani explains in her book Yurugu that this affirmation has the radical potential to destroy European hegemony:

"The implications of Maquet's proposed redefinition are radical in the context of the European utamawazo. A change that the phenomenologists have been attempting to effect for over a century. It would mean a complete break from the epistemology that is based on the idea and methodology of 'objectification,' on which the total separation of 'subject' and 'object'—of the 'knower' from the 'known'—is predicated. Ultimately, the implications of a radical change in the definition of knowledge or 'what it means to know' are not only a change in epistemological methodology, but a change in the European conception of the self, with corresponding changes in the conception of 'other' and behavior towards others as well. If the traditional mode of European science—'objectification'—loses its position of primacy on their scale of values, the redefinition of the culture itself theoretically becomes possible. But the utamaroho will not allow such a change. Any other conception would be inconsistent with the asili. The culture would be in basic conflict and therefore cease to function: it would not 'fit' its members.

"Change would have to occur at the most fundamental level; the level of the asili. We are talking about destruction. My suspicion is that neither Maquet nor the phenome- nologists are ready for anything that drastic. European thought is locked into an utamawazo in which 'science' plays a normative role. But there are questions to be answered: Why does science dominate? And why is science defined Eurocentrically? The ascendancy of science corresponds to other European characteristics and values. It supports a particular kind of monolith, the assurance of a particular kind of order, and behavior and development in a desired direction. These seem to have been Plato's 'reasons.' But what the illusion of objectification and the dominance of the scientific mode also succeed in doing is to allow Europeans to conceal their nationalistic objectives, e.g., their perspective. Scientism is science as ideology. It occurs when science becomes morality itself and, therefore, is above moral considerations."

Ultimately, Ani posits that once our bodies center our worldview, a new paradigm emerges, one that thoroughly displaces abstraction. Na'im Akbar, an African-centered psychologist, once remarked that a crucial tenant of Kemetic (ancient Egyptian) culture dictates that the body is a microcosm of the cosmos. This locates the substance of the world—and the universe—firmly in the body. Ergo, the more people understand themselves, the more they understand the world.

Here, history becomes paramount as our new reference point. Reflecting on the greatness of ancient African civilizations gives us a gateway out of the European cultural constructs that we often internalize to whitewash ourselves. Note that Pan-Afrikan nationalism's use of history differs starkly from the European take on history as a series of chronological events. The African cultural paradigm sees history as genealogical, indicative of a direct, on-going, living relationship with our past. Our active engagement with our ancestors allows us to lift ourselves out of the maze of European thought, and into our own set of ideas that account for how our bodies are situated in this world.

An African cultural paradigm requires a shift in foundation as well as focus. A cultural paradigm is neither scientifically nor biologically determined. It manifests through observation. A close reading of European, and by extension, American, history reveals an ethos based on discovering truth through science. Rationality trumps morality to benefit the privileged. Both past and present scientific studies have sought to establish the intellectual inferiority of Black people. Their spurious findings were then used to justify oppression, e.g., forced sterilization and population control. In ancient African civilizations, the people's welfare took precedence over rationality. Consider ma'at, an ancient African concept that locates truth squarely in the context of justice. Based on this principle, science that produces injustice cannot be truth, rendering mistreatment based on science fundamentally unjust.

Only within the European cultural paradigm could America unabashedly claim to be founded on justice in the midst of chattel slavery and indigenous genocide. The cognitive dissonance that accompanies this travesty directly results in the extreme level of abstraction and objectification endemic in European cultural thought. Pan-Afrikan nationalism injects us with the antidote to diseased thinking. Once cured, we can remove ourselves from the European historical narrative and navigate the world with a lens rooted in our own history and culture.

We cannot possibly thrive as objects in the dominant narrative, which holds that people of African descent have no history. G.W.F. Hegel writes:

"The peculiarly African character is difficult to comprehend, for the very reason that in reference to it, we must quite give up the principle which naturally accompanies all our ideas—the category of Universality. In Negro life the characteristic point is the fact that consciousness has not yet attained to the realization of any substantial objective existence —as for example, God, or Law—in which the interest of man's volition is involved and in which he realizes his own being. This distinction between himself as an individual and the universality of his essential being, the African in the uniform, undeveloped oneness of his existence has not yet attained; so that the Knowledge of an absolute Being, an Other and a Higher than his individual self, is entirely wanting. The Negro, as already observed, exhibits the natural man in his completely wild and untamed state. We must lay aside all thought of reverence and morality—all that we call feeling—if we would rightly comprehend him; there is nothing harmonious with humanity to be found in this type of character. The copious and circumstantial accounts of Missionaries completely confirm this, and Mahommedanism appears to be the only thing which in any way brings the Negroes within the range of culture."

Black people can scarcely flourish within an academy that has, from its inception, denied and ignored our history, while rendering us footnotes in the European socio-cultural universe. Our liberation will come through becoming our own nation managers, building our own institutions. From these strongholds, we can effectively advocate for policy reform. True justice is attained when we have the power to uplift ourselves. Disembodied theory, with the self as abstraction, hinders self-reliance because it ignores the body as our power source. Likewise, those of us committed to social justice disconnect the need for social transformation from our own personal transformations. Our transformations have taken shape through our work in Baltimore City, where we have dedicated ourselves to building independent Black power, the basis of Pan-Afrikan nationalism.

What is Black? The issue of essentialism

Pan-Afrikan nationalism overwrites prevailing European ideas of biological determinism. That people of African descent have different existential qualities from European descendants owes itself to divergent histories, not genetic makeup. An African cultural framework illuminates the essential quality in the universe as the spirit, that which animates the body. Spirit gives the world, and each life within it, meaning. We protect children, fall in love, and cry to honor the Divine, creator of all spirits. William Augustus Jones notes that "one's theology shapes one anthropology, which shapes your sociology." Our concept of God shapes our humanity, and by extension, how we order society. Rather than being mystical or anti-intellectual, recognizing the primacy of the spirit bespeaks an African cultural paradigm, whereas the European one deifies science. The god of scientific rationality is evident where societal development equals scientific achievement, as opposed to the betterment of people's quality of life. "Developed" nations have access to complex economic and scientific systems, irrespective of living conditions on an individual level. By rejecting scientific rationality and embracing a worldview like ma'at, we can harness our spiritual qualities to interpret the world, using the template of ancient African civilizations. Clarke asserts that "African societies did not have a word for jail because they didn't need a jail." Questioning whether and how such a practice could be implemented in modern America will help guide us out of the European cultural ethos.

If the world is essentially spiritual, then the essence of a people unifies them wherever they settle. The similarities among how Africans have structured societies globally transcends science. In place after place, we have used music as an integral method of evoking spiritual forces to fight against our oppression. In the U.S., we composed negro spirituals to endure and to escape chattel slavery. Black people created capoeira in Brazil as a martial art disguised as a dance to hide it from their slave masters. The rhythms of the West African-derived Vodun ceremony inspired the initial phases of the Haitian revolution. Again, these are not scientifically determined qualities of African people. We can observe African social systems across the diaspora to trace the inherent qualities of our people.

An essential African ethos does not translate into a static, singular brand of "Blackness." People of African descent can express their Africaness however they choose. Pan-Afrikan nationalism applies no litmus test, no one way to be Black. Liberal critiques of essentialism fall apart when Blackness is conceived as an orientation, not solely a biological identity. All of us directly descended from the African continent are legatees of a transgenerational historical memory passed down to each of us. Even those of us who are disconnected to our biological parents have within us a spiritual essence that is the gift of Blackness.

Class-first analysis

In order for Black people to reach our full, psychological potential, we must become self-actualized, have a healthy and strong knowledge and love of ourselves. Because of the centuries of sustained and targeted denigration of Africa, there are psychological affects of racism that require specific Black culturally based interventions that white people should not attempt to administer. It is better for us to organize ourselves based on an identity that gives us strength, as oppose to an identity that is rooted in being oppressed. We need institutions that affirm and support our development as whole human beings. Reading history as a series of class-based struggles obstructs these goals. Class-first analysis reiterates White supremacy by allowing White people to dictate to us how we should address our oppression. We must look to our African heritage for strength, but White people cannot be responsible for, or involved in, cultivating our new framework, not when Marxism governs the liberal academic machine, with proponents and opponents alike deploying class as the primary basis for struggle. Class is not "colorblind," and our Blackness is not an inconsequential accident but an important gift that needs to be cultivated.

Gender & Sexuality

Conversely, drawing from feminism and queer theory helps us to define Blackness wholly separate from White liberal masculinity. We can then displace the mainstream, hetero-normative rubric as the standard by which ways of being should be measured, such that straight Black men are not the arbiters of what constitutes Blackness. That said, in the academy, feminist and queer theory function as arguments against the development of independent Black institutions, instead of complements to how we build these institutions to embrace all people of African descent. They are, in fact, political movements based in White, disembodied ideas, deployed to coalesce the definition of Whiteness. While feminist and queer theory challenge our construction of Blackness in certain political formulations, they ultimately fail, in and of themselves, to answer how we build Black institutions.

We do concede that women and LGBT people of African descent are often excluded from leadership in struggle for freedom. In so doing, we have succumbed to a sexist, patriarchal socialization that imagines leadership as properly being exercised in the bodies of straight, Black men. This has two major implications. Firstly, we reproduce iterations of Blackness that violate Black women and Black LGBT people. Some Black nationalists equate establishing Black freedom with reclaiming their manhood and positioning women as appendages to men's lives, not autonomous individuals. In undermining Black women's agency, sexism contributes to a Black male sense of ownership over women's bodies. As with chattel slavery, so with sexism—when one person owns another, the "owner" can rationalize aggression toward any "property" that reaches beyond their station. Black LGBT people often confine their sexuality to the private sphere, under constant threat of violence for daring to display affection for same-sex partners publicly. Black men can be both sexist and homophobic, but we have internalized this violent, restrictive paradigm of gender identity and absorbed it into the cultural matrix of our people. Consequently, our commitment to hetero-sexism has impeded our ability to unify as a people to develop the independent institutions that we need.

Secondly, by refusing to see leadership outside of straight, male bodies, we perpetuate a cycle of sustaining bad leadership in two ways: by ignoring revolutionary thinkers and activists and by supporting cults of personality, as mentioned earlier. The ideas of Ella Baker, probably the most brilliant organizer the world has ever seen, are not heavily circulated, and thus we miss out on vital organizing lessons. So, too, does Bayard Rustin often escape notice, though he figured heavily in organizing during the Civil Rights Movement. To omit him is to miss out on his strategic knowledge and success. Concerning the "charismatic Black leader," this caricature promotes effective leadership as egocentric, sexist, and homophobic, now commonplace in today's political world. This style of leadership can be quite superficially attractive, but for grassroots organizing, it is ineffective at developing the relationships necessary for cohesion. Regrettably, such leaders heavily populate White, mainstream, popular culture. As Black people, when we subscribe to such a narrow view, we lose people like Baker, who gave us a non-hierarchal template for cultivating leadership amongst the grassroots. Baker taught us that we need a method of organizing under which the entire community is empowered to speak on their own behalf. Rejecting hereto-sexism expands our ability to incorporate effectively innovation from all grassroots sectors, essential to our achieving Black liberation.

Nationalism redefined

Looking beyond the grassroots to national identity, we find that Europe's relationship to nationhood contrasts greatly with that of ancient African cultures. Their hegemony draws its might from colonial sovereignty, exerting power over the earth, best represented in the act of staking a flag in the land to declare ownership. As people of African descent, we embrace what Clarke refers to as the "territorial state." This concept defines a nation by the people and their relationship to the territory from which people share culture and society. In ancient African societies, our relationship to the land grew out of cultural development and an axiology that were both mutually beneficial to all inhabitants of the land. Clarke remarks on the way in which the multiple cultures within a nation would fertilize and share with each other, in marked contrast with European nationhood, which requires assimilation into a singular national identity. Diop argues that there is a cultural unity amongst African peoples regardless of their particular ethnic and national differences, a unity reflected in many of the items mentioned above as part of the "African Cultural Paradigm."

For this reason, European iterations of nationhood cannot simply be projected onto nation-building within Pan-Afrikan nationalism. For instance, while Marcus Garvey uses the term "sovereignty" throughout his work, he calls for political and economic independence from Europe's legacy of colonial conquest, whereas

European sovereignty justifies that conquest. We can absolutely redefine mainstream terminology to reflect Pan-Afrikan nationalist ideals, yet the left uses scholars like Giorgio Agamben to discredit Garvey's use of the term sovereignty as not sufficiently radical. Moreover, under the guise of feminist critique, leftist academics accuse Pan-Afrikan nationalists of being uniquely sexist. Our call for sovereignty is misrepresented as patriarchal violence toward women. We deplore any Black men who engage in violent and patriarchal acts toward women and call themselves Pan-Afrikan nationalists, nor do we aspire to a male-centered state. Black men—and men in general—across the political spectrum harbor as much sexism as certain Pan-Afrikan nationalists. However, we will not allow them, or the academy, to impugn our legitimate aims with a minority view of subjugation that flies in the face of our very foundation.

The Negrophobia/Negrophilia Paradox and Liberal (Academic) White Supremacy

By Lawrence Grandpre

A (Not So) Beloved Community: The Debate Community as Framework for a Discussion of Liberalism Academic White Supremacy

One white male coach of the Resistance exemplified the fetishization of black debaters in grotesque ways. He was a very competitive person and tried very hard to motivate the students for success. This created tension because the debaters were clearly interested in more than competitive success and they had ethical limits concerning what they thought was appropriate to say and what they thought should not be said.

In interviews, this coach spoke about the effort of his students in telling ways. He stated that his 'dick gets so hard' when he comes across sharp literature from the black radical tradition that might be useful in debates. During the debate competition he

41

would pace the halls nervously. Once he saw me and was telling me how good one of the students was doing. He regularly had a sexual way of explaining things and even explained that when he hears one of the students speaking in militant poetic verse, 'it makes my dick hard.' In interviews he mentioned, and even expressed regret about this feature of his coaching. He admitted that at points he would establish a blackness meter and tell his students how 'black' they should act. Sometimes he would tell the students they need to 'coon it up' for a particular judge. His goal was to win at all costs and the students and their radicalism were his tools for doing so. Other coaches did this in a less blatant way but it was clear that they had an intense enjoyment of black speech as well. They would encourage more and more radicalism on the part of the students and suggest particular ways in which they should and could be more radical or militant. Students were also encouraged to deliver their speeches in (rap) form, even against the uneasiness they felt. Many students came to feel that their performances were feeding the white appetite to consume the spectacle of black suffering. Also, they felt trapped because

Consume Black suffering

42

they relied on these individuals for institutional support and could not easily criticize them.

University of California, Irvine Ph.D. David Peterson writing about a (former) Towson University debate teacher and coach

For four years I was an assistant debate coach for the Towson University debate team, a team made of predominantly black debaters, which specializes in using various strains of critical race theory in intercollegiate policy debate. My responsibilities included critiquing and improving student arguments and performances, supplementing student research, producing original research for debaters, traveling with students to regional and national debate tournaments, and coordinating team travel logistics. The person depicted in the above quote was head debate coach and my superior for two of those years. I first met him in 2008 when he served as a graduate assistant for the team and I was an undergraduate at Whitman College. The director of debate revoked his assistantship after he got into several altercations with the debate coach, but he returned to the team in 2011 after the previous director of debate, a longtime ally of the black debaters on the team who clashed with the administration for her stances, was removed from her position. His wife, a professor at the university and former coach of the now defunct speech team, was approached to serve as director of debate after the previous coach was removed. She agreed, bringing her husband in as the head coach of the debate team.

Despite never reaching the highest levels of competitive successes in the debate community as a debater or coach, he was well known in the debate community. While debating for and then coaching debate at a prestigious northeastern liberal arts college, he delivered notoriously provocative arguments, famously used finger puppets of well-known postmodern philosophers as part of a debate argument, and coached a team that incorporated sex positive feminism (compete with sex toy props) in competitive debate rounds. He was infamous for his direct, argumentative, and often abrasive demeanor, which was a manifestation of his proclaimed disregard for the established social norms and mores of the debate community. He seemed to be interested in radically challenging its basic assumptions to make more space for intellectual and political freedom.

This anti-establishment carried over to his self-proclaimed anti-racism. He would often accuse other white coaches as being insufficiently radical in their approaches to debate. He also presented himself as a white ally for people of color in the debate community. Upon returning to Towson debate in 2011, he spoke to me about his white privilege and committed to using his privileged status to secure resources for black students on the debate team. He thus framed himself as the quintessential "good white

good, white, liberal ally

liberal ally," making my experiences with him all the more frustrating and disappointing. I would observe this coach repeatedly verbally attacking students for not agreeing with his ideas, threatening their scholarships for not advancing his conception of proper deference and proper debating, intimidating students on the team, and having violent outbursts of anger, including throwing furniture.

Eventually, with help from alumni and debate coaches from other schools, students on the Towson team filed a threat incident report against this coach, leading to an investigation that eventually led to the coach's termination from both the debate coaching job and all teaching responsibilities on campus. This raises the questions: "What went wrong, and how could this happen?" After all, this coach and his wife (the director of debate at Towson University) had consistently asserted their "anti-racism." This paper seeks to use the answers to these questions as a template for evaluating white academic eurocentrism and white anti-blackness as a system that has gone largely unseen and vastly under theorized in the Academy. I argue that this is just one example of a liberal white supremacy that is just as or even more dangerous than the overt racism that is universally denounced in society today.

In order to understand this paper, in both content and style, it is necessary to understand a little about the college debate community. While the college policy debate community has long been seen as a training ground for

45

moderate/pragmatic policy makers, shifts in argumentative style have now made the community a unique place in which arguments from the contemporary liberal/ postmodern academic traditions are advanced and devolved in unique ways. Thus, the debate field has become a training ground for future feminist, queer studies, and race studies professors and future nonprofit workers. While academics in these categories often claim their respective academic disciplines have friendly disagreements or clashes with race scholarship, in the debate community, these arguments are clashed against one another in agonistic and sometimes antagonistic ways. It is consequently a unique space to observe how white liberal academics who call themselves "allies" deploy liberal academic scholarship *against* black students using critical race theory.

Some may feel this is an unrepresentative sample under artificial conditions, but I hope to show through a deep exploration of the roots of Eurocentric liberalism and my experiences in the debate community, larger academia and community activism, that the exact *opposite* is true. Such an examination of the dynamic of the Towson Debate team and the debate community en masse can be a useful way of seeing how the dynamics of liberal academia function in relation to policing and co-opting black thought and black bodies.

Introduction: With Friends Like These, Who Needs Enemies?

Liberal is one of the most complex words in the current political discourse. It is vilified in conservative media, glorified by the left, and generally misunderstood by everyone. However, young people tend to support ideas on the liberal end of the spectrum: support for liberal ideals like gay and interracial marriage, the need for anti-discrimination laws in the workplace, and less punitive drug policy. Thus, the notion that academic liberalism can serve to support oppression and white supremacy is counterintuitive to most people in general and young people in particular.

In my experience, many young people find the introduction to liberal values eye-opening after growing up in conservative households or conservative parts of the country, and credit their engagement with feminist, Marxist, and progressive teachers with a renewed sense of political responsibility and commitment to equality. While many African American students are from nominally/politically liberal environments (i.e., their parents and peers tend to vote democrat), they often, like myself, have been introduced to cultural conservatism/apolitical thought via black religious traditions and black capitalism/consumerism (both of which can be considered dominant thought systems in many black families). These students thus find engagement with liberal academics in college an enlightening experience.

This paper does not discount the reality of experiences for white and black students, but will seek to show their limitations and hidden costs. It is in recognition of how counterintuitive this argument may seem to many readers that I have tried to present this argument in detailed, systemic, yet assessable fashion by integrating personal experience, academic writings and speeches.

This piece will also pull from African centered philosophers and contemporary/historical critical race theorists to show the real world applications of seemingly abstract liberal philosophical ideas. The basic assumptions of power and freedom that are produced through the liberal academic studies of race will exhibit great significance in the functioning of political systems dominated by white liberalism and its conceptions of black suffering, specifically the nonprofit/left-activist communities. As such, this piece attempts to fulfill basic tenets of critical race theory: to use academic study as a tool for political analysis and to produce meaningful/useful conclusions to help oppressed people navigate oppression. I aim to reflect these goals by avoiding dense academic language where possible and attempting to show material examples of the dangers of liberal academic views of blackness. I would also like to propose productive ways of studying blackness and, more importantly, concrete examples for black people most affected by liberal racism so that they can survive, subvert, and strategically appropriate these dynamics to their advantage.

Crit. race theory

A few clarifying remarks. First, this piece stems from my unique experiences as an activist/educator. While I have intimate experience with the academy and as a coach in the world of college and high school debate, I have also spent a substantial period of time over the past five years working on political ventures in the city of Baltimore. Because I have not been in a formal academic setting as a student in five years, my insights are as an outsider reflecting upon the academy, and while I will try to follow academic codes of best practices, this piece will also pull largely from personal experiences and should be seen outside any disciplinary framework and outside of traditional notions of scholarly decorum or respectability. The goal is to communicate as clearly as possible a power dynamic that I have personally observed, using scholarship to clarify how these concerns are not new but are longer standing concerns addressed by (often overlooked) black scholars. Second, this piece will use the terms *Eurocentric* and *white* somewhat interchangeably, but the author finds it important to note that black and non-white teachers and theorists can also replicate Eurocentric thinking with how they approach blackness. This examination is thus not exclusive to white teachers and white liberals, but stems largely from experiences of white academics and white liberals.

Definition of Terms: Race's Role in Defining Liberalism

In order to nail down such a slippery term like liberalism, it is necessary to see how what we call "political liberalism" stems from a European philosophical tradition. European philosophical liberalism is very different than

American political liberalism, and seeing how their differences evolved is an essential starting point for critiquing white liberalism in the academy.

For hundreds of years, European liberal philosophy has attempted to produce a theory for thought and social organization that prioritizes the rights and freedom of individuals living in a mutually beneficial social contract, while simultaneously ignoring the violent, racist social foundations that made this so-called free society possible. While it is difficult to narrow classic European philosophical liberalism into a single static definition, this school of thought generally classifies the individual as the essential unit of sociopolitical life. Given the inevitable conflict between individuals, the state comes into being through agreements between individuals (i.e., the social contract) to mediate tensions, establish rights to protect basic freedoms, and develop themselves though economic, political, or social activity.

Within this framework, assumptions about (1) the ability of the state to impartially adjudicate disputes between these abstract liberal subjects, (2) the desire for the subjects to operate individually (versus collectively) in the political sphere, (3) the assumed shared notions of freedom, and (4) the fact that all stakeholders have played an equal part in developing the social contract, all create weaknesses within a system that will reproduce inequalities if unchecked—even though European liberal philosophy was designed to treat everyone equally. It is this possibility that leads Northwestern University professor Charles Mills to wonder:

> But what if—not merely episodically and randomly but systematically and structurally—the personhood of some persons was historically disregarded and their rights disrespected? What if entitlements and justice were, correspondingly, so conceived of that the unequal treatment of these persons, or subpersons, was not seen as unequal, not flagged as an internal inconsistency, but accommodated by suitable discursive shifts and conceptual framings? And what if, after long political struggles, there developed at last a seeming equality that later turned out to be more nominal than substantive, so that justice and equal protection were still effectively denied even while being triumphantly proclaimed? It would mean that we would need to recognize the inadequacy of speaking in the abstract of liberalism and contractarianism.

Of course, Mills does not merely speak in hypotheticals but explains the historical conditions by which liberal theory was marshaled to (re)produce white supremacy.

A good example of this is European philosopher John Locke. Locke is known as one of the fathers of liberalism. He claimed that individuals deserve the right to have the freedom to work and benefit from their labor in order to better themselves and society without undue interference from other individuals or the state. While this desire for freedom can be seen as positive in the abstract, it raises the question of what this freedom allows. For Locke and many other classical liberals, freedom was reserved for rich, white male capitalists to under seat rich white male feudal lords, monarchs, and religious leaders as dominate forces in European societies. This attitude stemmed from the notion that they had earned their success through merit and hard work, and should thus be free to climb the social ladder. These capitalists differentiated themselves from men who gained their positions solely by birthright.

This starts to expose the scandal at the heart of liberal theory: it was not some altruistic desire to expand freedom to a universal humanity that produced the birth of liberalism, as is often portrayed, but is instead what Mills calls "racial liberalism." The liberalism of today, which supports the freedom to live, think, love, and worship how we choose, is an essential corollary to the ideology that allowed white Europeans to believe that they should be free to profit from slavery (as Locke did), take Native American lands, and colonize Africa. Black and brown people did not count in the liberal social contract, as they were not *subjects* of liberal theory, but *objects*.

Even today, to the extent that liberalism has been seen as helping black people, this view of liberalism's history shows these seemingly positive results stem not

52

from any sense of altruism, but out of self-interest for white liberals. Former Harvard University professor Derek Bell popularized the concept of *interest convergence*, arguing that many of the "successes" of the civil rights movement (i.e. Brown vs. Board of Education), should be seen through the lens of what positive benefits those in power (the government) garnered by advancing a legal agenda against segregation and improving their standing in the eyes of the world which facilitated American propaganda efforts during the Cold War. The perception of supporting freedom was a useful tool America could wield against the Soviet Union, and thus the elimination of segregation allowing America to advance its global agenda. Similarly, the Civil Rights Act and limited desegregation allowed America to promote a capitalist economy that could benefit even the most downtrodden, creating a useful image for a country advancing capitalism as an ideology of freedom. Contrast this with socialism, which was depicted as the state forcing wealth redistribution through high taxes and limiting freedom through state managed economics. Thus, the seeds for the shortcomings of the Civil Rights Movement were sowed in the Europe of John Locke: for just as an abstract ideology of personal freedom can justify slavery and imperialism, it also prohibits corrective measures such as reparations and affirmative action from being considered. Such measures would violate the freedom of privileged people. It is important to note that whether steps such as affirmative action are seen as just or fair stem from one's perception of society. Eurocentric

53

liberalism has monopolized our perceptions to the point that it influences American political discourse on both the right and the left.

This also hints at what could be called an epistemological critique of the process of liberalism, with epistemology being a term used to describe the process by which individuals (and societies) produce knowledge. To clarify, let's again turn to John Locke. Locke asserts that Native Americans did not have a legitimate claim to their lands because they left them unimproved (e.g. without sophisticated farms or other European advancements). This is not only a racist assumption about the fundamental laziness of Native Americans, but it is also factually incorrect. Much of what Europeans saw as virgin forest in the New World was actually, according to University of Arizona professor Gary Nabhan, second growth forest, or trees that had regrown after years of deforestation for farming and other uses. Native Americans had farms, complex governing structures, and highly planned out migratory patterns, but none of their systems registered in the white academy of the day, which viewed them as "noble savages" to be either killed or saved via religious conversion.

Native americans stripped of land rights

What is important to note in framing this as an epistemic argument rather than a moral failing is that even if all Europeans did not have bad intentions toward Native Americans or Africans, the argument is that Europeans were fundamentally limited by the cognitive frames (or mental templates for making sense of the world) they had for interpreting reality. In relation to Native Americas and Africans, for example, the lack of clearly defined individually demarked plots of land lead Europeans to believe they had no relationship with the land that need be respected, i.e. they had no clear signs of individual private property. The real complexity of the relationship people of color had with the land could simply not be seen by the even the "enlightened" Europeans due to their unfamiliarity with the land in question and inability to conceptualize an idea like *communal* ownership due to the European, individualist, "liberal" foundation of their moral systems.

That the European liberal tradition proclaims freedom and equality for all on paper yet in practice produces global subjugation is a contradiction of Mill's claims. He fails to take a stab at answering the difficult, emotionally laden question of *why* European liberalism evolved this way and instead focuses his conservable talents on explaining *how* racial liberalism functions. Marimba Ani in her book *Yurugu* gives critical insight into the cultural foundations behind the seemingly contradictory liberal impulses of freedom and subjugation, writing in a passage that deserves to quoted at length:

> It has been part of the posture of the moral philosophers of European culture to disavow cultural commitment, yet their work has contributed significantly to the survival and intensification of the rhetorical ethic-the hypocrisy and the deception that constitute a

vital and definitive part of the content of European cultural imperialism-and, therefore, to nationalistic objectives. To begin with the Platonic-influenced utamawazo provides the theoretical basis for a conceptual ethics; an ethical system, the themes of which are considered to be valid, as long as they are consistent in terms of the logic of that system. What is 'ethical' becomes what is 'rational' and 'logical.' The most 'ethical' statement is the purest abstraction. As Havelock correctly observes, the individual 'thinking' psyche becomes the seat of morality and the individual's ability to act ethically is based on his ability to think 'rationally'; i.e., 'abstractly.'

So long as they work for white supremacy

The result, again, is 'talk.' The European idea is that words divorced from action, feeling, commitment, from human involvement can themselves be relevant to (and properly inform) human interaction-as long as they are part of a consistent syntax; an approved semantic system. This pursuit itself is an exercise in self-deception. Primary cultures are characterized by an 'existential ethic' (Stanley Diamond) that is based on and refers to actual behavior. European culture gives rise to semantic

words are divorced from action

"approved symantic system" by white pavee

systems and instead of being concerned with the inconsistency between 'word' and 'deed' (which could conceivably be the determinant of ethical behavior), the moral philosophers are merely concerned with verbal and what they call 'logical' inconsistency. One result of this characteristic of the culture is a tendency to make philosophers the most irrelevant of people and to effectively divorce their work from any decision-making capacity or role that in any way influences the ethical behavior of European peoples. What this tradition has done instead is to support the culture in its ability to use words without meaning, and to support Europeans in their quest to deceive others and themselves as well. The body of literature known as 'ethical theory' has to a large degree been conducive to the growth of moral hypocrisy in European culture. It is the 'liberal' academic tradition in contemporary European/ European American culture that uses the rhetorical ethic best to support the objectives of European chauvinism. Ingeniously, these theorists use the semantical systems of the moral philosophers, the 'brotherhood' rhetoric of the Christian statement and empty

[handwritten margin note: not so much concerned w/ deed]

abstractions like 'humanitarianism' and 'universalistic ethics' as evidence of the ideological commitments of the Europeans and therefore as indices of the nature of European culture. They are 'critical,' because they say that the imperialistic behavior of the European has represented a conflicting theme or 'negative' tendency in European development. The result of their theories, however, is that they succeed in making the European responsible for everything-the 'good' as well as the 'bad'- and in the end the good far outweighs the bad and will, of course, triumph along with 'reason.'

Ani isolates a few essential characteristics of European thought that are essential to grounding a critique of contemporary white academic liberalism engagements of blackness. By couching European liberal ethical theory as "rhetorical ethics," she creates a framework (one of the very few in all of academia) that explains the contradiction at the heart of liberalism: if European ethics are grounded in a cultural impulse for producing pure abstractions to show intellectual and moral superiority of European liberal subjects, then ethical theory has become divorced from any material accountability (thus allowing slavery, imperialism, and native genocide to go unregistered). Consequently, Europe gives itself credit for inventing "real ethics" and thus has declared itself superior and has justified its violence and imperialism by bringing so-called enlightenment and freedom to the world. One need look no further than Iraq and Afghanistan to see contemporary examples of liberal ethics gone wrong, but this is also manifested in more insidious ways, like neoliberal economic policies that grace devolved countries with "economic freedom" from government intervention in markets (and consequently many of the essential services the government provides). Ani provides a historical example of missionaries bringing the truth of Christianity's message of a personal relationship with God (rather than a communal relationship in many indigenous cultures) and the promise of individual salvation.

This disjunction between Eurocentric worldviews and Ani's Africa-centered philosophy can be brought to life by comparing Rene Descartes' famous statement *cogito ergo sum* (or *I think therefore I am*) and the African proverb *I am because we are.* African psychologist Na'im Akbar uses this comparison as part of his critique of Eurocentric psychology's focus on personal introspection versus putting individuals into productive social contexts as a form of counseling. This comparison also serves as a good conceptual framework for a critique of Eurocentric liberalism; a Eurocentric frame for political engagement is not only fundamentally abstract and rhetorical, but individualistic in ways that make it difficult to conceptually engage the reality of people who have been oppressed as a group and, according to Ani and many other theorists, have historical roots of thinking in with the group and the individual as the primary frame for engaging the world.

While this may seem to be a minute point in the context of an archaic philosophical discussion, I believe it is impossible to overstate the importance of this finding: much of what the academy assumes to be objective truth in its study of people of color is actually an attempt to apply Eurocentric criteria where it does not belong. This allows the lives and experiences of oppressed people to make the most sense to white/Eurocentric academic thought and disregards the actual experiences of oppressed people. In the academy, Texas A&M professor Tommy Curry calls this "epistemic convergence," in which the academic work and lived experience of black people get interpreted in ways that assume Eurocentric criteria versus African centered criteria. I would add that scholarship, which fails to offer such epistemic convergence, like much of Black Nationalist or African centered scholarship, is simply ignored altogether or is branded as "not real scholarship." As the previous chapter on the dismissal of African centered/radical black scholarship (Pan-Africanism defined) suggests, it is really a code word for saying "not white scholarship" or "scholarship not useful for white interests."

black experience is explained through white language — rather than African

60

Two Sides of the Same Coin: Negrophilia and Negrophobia Explained

My critique of liberal academy will center on the ideas of negrophobia (from the Greek *phobia* for *fear*) and negrophilia (from the Latin *philia* for *love*), which are concepts grounded in the works of Franz Fanon and other critical race theorists. These concepts are also expanded upon by University of California-Irvine Professor Frank Wilderson. Whereas there is no binary opposition between negrophilia and negrophobia, seeing them as opposing sides of the same coin (in this case, the general desire to abstract black existence outside of its lived, material, human context and into an abstract, ideological context) is useful for understanding the working of the liberal academy. True to the ethos of this project, Wilderson's clear exposition of negrophobia and negrophilia comes not from his academic writings, but from an interview he did in 2011 talking on the World Cup and his personal experiences. Wilderson states:

> I traveled to Morocco and once I was traveling with a very light [skinned] black women, and I could not go in and get a hotel anywhere in Morocco. And the taxi driver got tired of this and said: "This woman that

you're with speaks French. Put a head rag on her so her afro is covered, have her go into the hotel that we just went into, have her order a room and then I can go home for the night."

He was tired of driving us all around. And it worked. By speaking French she could present herself as Arab, and my presence was immediately established as Senegalese. So, one of the things that everyone seems to know or everyone around the world, whether it's Basra in Iraq or in Spain or whether it's Agader in Morocco that we people, these people in these various countries, have a problem with white supremacy, okay, once white supremacy has been dealt with, the society still has, as its essential element, anti-blackness. And so I try to splice, splice a meditation on white supremacy, from a meditation on anti-blackness. Without anti-blackness, you don't have a world, anywhere. That's my argument. And I think that, anti-blackness, bringing it to the World Cup, can take again, building on Fanon, two kinds of trajectories. One trajectory is negrophobia, which is absolute fear of the presence of blacks in our space. The other trajectory is negrophilia.

[handwritten margin note: anti-blackness, not just white supremacy]

[handwritten margin note: w/o anti-blackness, you don't have a world anywhere]

Which is like, collecting little Negro objects for your shelf (laughing). You know. And negrophilia: "I just *love* black music," "I just *love* black people," "I just *love* African dancing," "I just *love* African soccer." Negrophilia is the other side of the same coin as negrophobia. They are mobilized by a paradigmatic condition in which the slave, or the black, is available gratuitously; the slave or the black is available gratuitously to the uses of others. Whether it is for the use of lynching, or for the use of pleasure. Negrophobia and negrophilia are the two twin modalities of anti-blackness that are… it's not a discriminatory issue, you can't do legislation against it, negrophobia and negrophilia are absolutely necessary to the coherence and stability of any society on this planet and without that you don't have a world. And this is why our problem is an antagonism, this is why the sports figure making multiple millions of dollars, have the same problem as Oscar Grant here in Oakland, whose on his back shot and killed. The same problem. They are both objects of the world; they are both not subject[s] in the world.

The notion that one can simultaneously be against white supremacy and support anti-blackness, like the notion of liberalism supporting oppression, may at first seem counterintuitive but ultimately makes sense. First, it is important for both Fanon and Wilderson that the concept of "collective psychology" is taken seriously, in terms of both that of the oppressing group and the oppressed group, despite the liberal desire to focus on individual difference, as sharing at some basic level certain social perspectives that limit and shape the scope the group members views of themselves and the world. Its goal is not to study the nuances of individual traumas and sexual repression/desires to understand personal problems (as in the traditional Eurocentric model) but to see how deep-seated, widespread, and socially reinforced psychological concepts of race affect the lived experience of black and white people worldwide. Wilderson's analysis reveals "anti-blackness" as the psychological foundation that undergirds both the love of black people and the hatred of them. In both cases, black people are taken not as they are in the historical and cultural context, but instead are abstracted *never* into ideas and placed into a system of thought. For the *fully* negrophobe, these ideas are coded with negative *human* characteristics; for the negrophile, these same ideas are coded with good characteristics. In both cases, black people are objects to be projected upon and are objects that serve the purposes of the projectors. In both cases, black people are never fully human.

The remainder of this paper will provide contextual examples of how these two dynamics operate in my personal experience. However, given how central these dynamics are to this chapter, it may be helpful to review a case study of how the negrophilia/negrophobia paradox functions. Following Wilderson's lead with the World Cup example, the world of sports shows how perceptions of black people are often contradictory. In the ESPN documentary "Ghosts of Ole Miss," the tale of a successful, all-white University of Mississippi football team is juxtaposed with the story of the university's first black student, James Meredith. The film discusses specific instances of racist incidents in Mississippi and shows how football was finally integrated at the school in the 1970s. Like many top football teams during this era, Ole Miss soon featured a majority black team with a majority white fan base. While hitting on a few larger social issues, the documentary largely frames this as an example of social progress and tolerance, and thus reaffirms the standard liberal narrative that through hard work and rationality, racism can be alleviated and justice can be secured. After all, the African American players overcame and avoided the bias of white coaches by proving they were superior through training and preparation, winning scholarships, and showing the potential for lucrative professional football careers.

An analysis of negrophilia/negrophobia would question such a liberal narrative. After all, if acceptance on the football field reflected social progress, it is unclear why blacks in Mississippi are specifically at or near the bottom compared to the rest of the United States when it comes to many indicators of social welfare (such obesity rates, child poverty, and educational attainment), according to a 2014 report published by The Annie E. Casey Foundation called *Race for Results*. The cheering of the white fans, in this framework, is a form of otherization, in which the fans are receiving enjoyment out of experiencing the "super human" power of black athletes. Through their affiliation with the liberal state and the institution of the university, white fans view themselves as having control over the players versus respecting and appreciating them as people. This framework proposes that white fans are projecting their own desires for strength and power onto the players, which in fact dehumanizes and creates caricatures of black athletes.

This interpretation is supported by the work of University of Texas at Austin professor John Hoberman. He explains in his 2006 essay *Race and Athletics in the 21st Century* and his 1996 book *Darwin's Athletes* the long history of projecting super human strength and pain tolerance upon the black body that dates back to slavery. These projections have produced a social myth about black athletic superiority, which, in addition to poverty, then pushes black men and women into sports due to a perceived lack of other opportunities. Consequently, blacks are kept in more socially acceptable roles as workhorses and entertainers who channel their innate animalistic impulses Sub-human into something constructive. Fans' love of black athletes

Perceived lack of opportunities – turn to sports

66

serves as the flip side of negrophobia; if blacks are to be super human, animalistic and impulsive, it is best to keep them under the control of someone "trustworthy" who can [coaches] help channel their intensity in the service of order, productivity, or entertainment.

To further drive home this point, Richard King in *Behind the Cheers: Race as Spectacle in College Sports* asserts that white fans continued to wave the confederate flag at Ole Miss football games well into the 1970s, even when more than half of the football team was black. Conservative blogger Paul Kersey interprets this as proof that the rebel flag was not a symbol of white supremacy and that the liberal theory of race relations has a hard time proving otherwise, since support for black football players is seen as a rational evolution away from the racist views of the past. The negrophilia/negrophobia paradox reveals the cheering of the fans to be not a reputation of their past racism, but an evolution. Hobberman and many others have pointed out that National Football League prospects are evaluated in a method very similar to that of slaves—made to strip down to their underwear, undergo examinations of their physiques, and perform athletic drills (only to play not for the team of their choice, but for the team that selects them during the draft). When this logic is applied to the concept of spectatorship, the frightening thought of white fans placing themselves in the metaphorical position of slave owners gleefully evaluating their property projects a very serious shadow over what at first glance seems like a fun escape.

"Racial advancement"
Liberals saying
or look they are succeeding

The liberal logic that would see the possibility of a professional football career and a college scholarship as an example of racial advancement is severely undermined by this argument in theory, and a bevy of growing popular criticism about the NFL shows that this theory holds in practice. In the NFL, only a small section of most players' salaries are guaranteed, with players subject to termination whenever the team sees fit, including in the face of serious injury. The NFL also lacks adequate long-term medical coverage despite the extremely violent nature of the sport and its proven relationship to head trauma (as fans' love of athletes does not seem to extend to caring for them after they are no longer assets).

At the collegiate level, the free education players receive in theory is fundamentally undermined in practice because it prevents athletes from being compensated for their athletic achievements while under scholarship. This forces college athletes to suffer financial hardship and sets them up for severe punishment if they were to be caught using their status to improve the lives of themselves or their families. Numerous grading and cheating scandals shows many schools advising players to take easier classes in order to stay academically eligible and provide more time for athletic training, which fundamentally undermines the quality of their education in the name of maximizing their usefulness to the team and earning power for the school. *← white*

More than one player has compared college football directly to slavery, and while recent moves seem to trend toward elite college athletes, the story of Jermane Clarke most clearly reveals the reality negrophobia crashes down upon this mythology of liberal progress. A former North Carolina A&T football player, Mr. Clarke got into a car crash and knocked on a nearby door for assistance. Thinking the physically imposing black man to be a criminal, the young white women in the house called the cops, who upon arrival, shot the unarmed Clarke and killed him. This reveals in stark detail what Wilderson means when he makes the seemingly counter intuitive statement that Oscar Grant, the unarmed young man shot while handcuffed in the subway in Oakland, and a football star have the same *essential political problem*. The adulation the sports stat, in this case Clarke, receives is contingent upon a societal view of blackness that otherizes him, and reaffirms basics assumptions about black physicality that naturalizes his status as a threat. This reveals a fundamental limitation in liberal theories on race, the prioritization of emotional, personal/individual pronouncements, and seemingly altruistic actions—like a white family taking in a poor black athlete (who happened to play at the University of Mississippi) in the now famous book/movie *The Blind Side* while ignoring the structural and historical realities of anti-blackness necessary to put these actions into context. Personal educational and emotional evolution is seen as the solutions to racism, obscuring the legacies of slavery that continually manifest themselves in social institution, from the fields Oxford, Mississippi to the streets of Ferguson, Missouri.

This concept of negrophilia/negrophobia is essential to understanding the events in this chapter and, more importantly, contemporary American racism in general. So often people are confused by a world where a black man can be president and, at the same time, black people are being gunned down in racially-motivated shootings. In the liberal model of race, this is a contradiction, but when viewing the world through the lens of negrophobia and negrophilia, these two events can logically co-exist and even logically support one another. This paper does not claim to be an exhaustive analysis of all the nuances of how this dynamic operates. The similarities and differences in terms of how this paradox affects black bodies is an issue beyond the scope of this paper. However, it does serve as a conceptual framework to go beyond the liberal framework and to begin to see how it can become a tool to replicate racism and white supremacy.

Case Studies in the Negrophilia/Negrophobia Paradox: Debate and Beyond

An analysis of the debate community, academia, and politics in Baltimore reveals the dangers of the liberal academic negrophilia/negrophobia paradox. By viewing these three areas not separate but as connected through their shared liberalism can see common threads of anti-blackness we think through the institutions engagement with black theory and black bodies as framed through the Negrophilia Negro phobia paradox. This section will

70

attempt to show comment responses to all three institutions, with liberal politics/ nonprofits as the material embodiment of the abstract anti-black racism theorized in the white Eurocentric academy.

A common foundational problematic down through all three of these institutions is the inability to see black suffering as a material reality to be engaged, but instead an abstract sought to be theorized about and placed into a Eurocentric system of thought. Many people would be surprised to know the personal characteristics of the coach discussed in the quote at the beginning of this paper. He in many ways is the epiphany of a "good white liberal academic". He talked constantly of his affinity for black art, black music, and black radical political theory. He would often openly express his disdain for other coaches who were in his mind were "bad white liberals" and "faux antiracists". As the quote suggests, he constantly promoted students evolution as political radicals, encouraging them to be more radical in their political thinking and debate style. So how could someone who seemingly was doing so much "correct" go so wrong?

The answer to this question using the foundational problematic of Eurocentric thought outlined by Ani, the epistemic frame used to evaluate black suffering turned it into an abstraction that prevents even well-meaning white educators from correctly interpreting the reality of white supremacy and thus prevents them from effectively teaching and engaging black students. For example, the coach would consistently make comments about the plight of "poor blacks in the ghetto" failing to realize that many of his students, including myself as a coach, would have fallen into this category in the past, or more problematically, would still fall into this category in the present. In his coaching the coaching question word become excited at the prospect of using the debaters experiences with black suffering as tools to defeat their opponents, instructing them to "keep it real", a term he would use to denote his desire for the students to give personal testimonies of a life under the oppression of poverty and racism as a tool to undermine their opponents' philosophical abstractions. This would on facing in to be in accordance with the goal of this paper, however the problematic is shown when the coaches practices reveal its fundamental inability to take the reality of poverty and racism that he instructed his debaters to talk about in debate into account in his personal coaching practices. The coach consistently complained to me about the debaters being late to practice, being distracted at practice, sign he saw as proof the debaters were "not committed to debate". This would lead him to verbally assault the debaters, threatening their scholarships and personally attacking the character on several occasions. Impact of incredible cognitive dissonance, the coach after verbally berating his debaters would often proceed to give them rides home dropping them off in Baltimore city communities that were often very impoverished, violence filled, and lacking resources, facts that seemed to completely alleviated the coach when he made the shortcomings of the debaters a matter of personal failings rather than the structural conditions in which they lived. The reality of the situation was that these debaters were dealing with life obstacles completely beyond the coaches epistemological frame of understanding; they would be late to practice not necessarily because of their lack of commitment, but because they would have to take a bus 90 minutes each way to get the practice. They will be distracted not necessarily because they were uninterested in their arguments or in debate, but because each of these debaters were dealing with internal strife at home including parental sickness, caring for siblings, incarcerated siblings, personal finance problems, and other conditions that should have registered in the coaches mind before he claimed that the debaters were lacking commitment. It is thus revealed that the coach constructed a reality wherein the material implications of racism white supremacy were occurring in the abstract to "those people in the ghetto", and not to students he coached or myself, shielding him from having to engage the emotional reality that people he was directly engaging and affecting or being influenced by the violence he theorized.

This mirrors Eurocentric academia as shuttle tendency to engage black suffering as an abstraction rather than a reality. A friend of mine who was attending an elite undergraduate university reported that in thesis defense in which he focused on the dehumanization suffered by black people under racism, a member of his thesis defense committee responded "what about the suffering of animals?" The implication here is that by using the category of "the human" that my friend was tacitly replicating the violence done by humans against the environment. When suffering becomes abstracted, Eurocentric academia response to the suffering was more abstractions, including a concern that these investigations was suffering in the abstract different forms of suffering (such as animals suffering), a response which serves to of absolve oneself of personal responsibility to engaging the reality of suffering being presented in the first place.

A link can be drawn between the abstraction of black suffering and the Academy and real political impacts. In my work with LBS one of our main campaigns was to stop the construction of a proposed youth jail in Baltimore city. The argument was that the current status of his incarceration was inhumane, and use warehouse in aging facilities and alongside dangerous adult offenders. Thus a $104 million incarceration facility was proposed to house youth charged as adults. This placed an argument traditionally seen as conservative, the building of more jails, within a "liberal" political framework, as the jail would improve living conditions for youth charged as adults as compared to the status quo situation. Our argument as LBS was that the money that would be invested in this facility would be better spent on preventative engagement programs and community-based rehabilitation which what's solve the overcrowding problem and provide opportunities for those in the community doing use rehabilitation and advocacy work to get access to the resources while keeping the youth in the community rather than incarcerated. In our work we found that white liberals consistently responded, "I don't understand. Why would you be against improving prison conditions?" The suffering of the prisoners in their minds had been abstracted to simply "the conditions in prison are bad," while our conception of black suffering was far more expansive, including the suffering of use charged as adults in the first place, being removed from their communities, being systemically denied opportunities for reintegration and social advancement, and the persistent denial of culturally competent services. By adopting a more expansive vision of black suffering, LBS was able to have a more extensive intellectual toolkit when it came to proposing solutions for use incarceration, while the extracted vision of suffering produced by white academic liberalism and thus exported into the nonprofit community limited conceivable solutions to "better prisons", thus serving to perpetuate the prison industrial complex and white supremacy.

A more in-depth examination of the logic of white liberals shown in the youth jail by reveals another dynamic of the Negrophilia/Negro phobia paradox. We often heard white liberals speak about youth being attacked or indoctrinated by fellow prisoners as one of the central problems to be addressed in the debate over the youth jail. A "objective" analysis of the conditions of black youths would reveal systemic poverty, failed schools, racialized policing tactics, bias in sentencing practices, and other systemic factors as being more salient and discussion overproduced justice. So why did so many white liberals frame fellow inmate as potential threat? As an interrogation of the debate community shows, there is a tendency within the Eurocentric epistemic framework to frame other blacks as the potential threat to black communal advancement, rather than white supremacy or white people. The paradox here is that, within the Eurocentric imaginary, the love of blackness/black people is manifested through protecting black people from other, non-enlightened Blacks. Here again, experiences from the Towson debate team prove illustrative. The head coach, a self-proclaimed follower of the theories of philosopher Giles Deleuze and his admonishment against having fixed/static views of the world, would often make derogatory comments about the "essentialist" or "non-scholarly" analysis of other black coaches or debaters. In one glaring example, the coaching question chastised one of the debaters for being too close to her high school debate coach, saying "I think I know enough about black people to say that he has a Napoleon complex". The context for this moment is important, as the dispute was about whether the arguments the Towson debater's high school coach was giving advice that counted as high quality scholarship, with the Towson debate coach insinuating that these arguments were more about a young black man's personal ego than about good debate strategy, claiming that only by combining black scholarship was postmodern Eurocentric scholarship would the debater be successful in college debate. Similarly, the Towson debate coach with make comments about a black, gay debate coach from another school, claiming "I know as a white male I'm not supposed to make these types of comments about black people, but he is a black gay ass hole". In both instances, the Towson debate coach uses his asserted antiracism as an inoculation against claims to be a racist, and positions himself as the appropriate middle ground between black male excess and "bad" whiteness. While these quotes may seem extreme, they mirror the white/ Eurocentric academies engagement with blackness. Ironically, the Towson debate coach would often coach teams to defeat other debaters use of theorists such as Paul Gilroy and others who claim that the arguments presented by Towson debate actually increased racism by treating race as real (and not a social construction); he would instruct his debaters to claim these arguments were a form of colorblind racism, yet failed to see how he personally performed the exact same colorblind racism he coached his debaters to defeat, giving a contextual example of what Ani would call the "moral hypocrisy" endemic to Eurocentric thought.

This antagonistic framing for antiracism resulted in coaching which often served the exact opposite effect of its intent. Once, when attempting to theorize responses to a team that talked about their religion, the head coach offered the idea of "why not just have the boys pretend to be Muslim and claim to be offended that other team would speak on their religion". The head coach relented when I pointed out that is represented a form of unethical scholarship, but not because of the perceived commodification of Islam, but because I framed the opposition as pragmatic claiming "the boys won't agree to that". Similarly, while I personally adopted a coaching ethic of not writing speeches for debaters, the head coach would often write scripts and notes for debaters, one that reflected his personal views on scholarship and not the debater's views. One example of the problem with this was when coach constructed an argument about coding identity and how it was violent to impose one conception of identity onto someone else. In was within this context that a quote from black spoken word poet Saul Williams' poem "Coded Language" was incorporated into the debate speech. The coach's intellectual framework for the argument meant the only section of the poem that "fit" this argument was the portion where Williams critiques the black communities fetishization of authenticity or "keeping it real" as a limit on acceptable black performance, and the rest of the poem finishes with the poet critiquing larger white society and white supremacy. Similarly, view the larger text of the poem and Williams' visual performance of the piece on HBO's *Def Comedy Jam* reveal how selecting only this portion of the poem obscures the author's intent. In his performances of the piece, Williams ironically mimics the style of a colonial era court official, unraveling long, white scroll and coaching each of his lines of poetry as a "whereas" clause, as in his first line: "Whereas, breakbeats have been the missing link connecting the diasporic community to its drum woven past."

This couches his apiece as a critique of traditional, formal legal discourse, and thus making said piece more amenable to a critique of traditional debate practices than black "identity policing". He also unbuttons his shirt to reveal a tea shirt with an outline of the continent of Africa, and goes on to call upon the spirit of many Black elders and traditional African deities, along with elders, events, and deities from a myriad of cultures, to advance the poems message of spiritual enlightenment in the face of oppression. The selective editing of the piece obscures the reality that his poem could just as easily be seen as linking him with a black aesthetic tradition as with a, for lack of a better term, "post black" aesthetic freedom against "hegemonic" notions of black identity. Thus, the intellectual framing of the argument produces a framework where black artists and intellectual become tools to be deployed against the perceived threat "unenlightened" notions black identity, assuage white academic fears that these ideas reflect Eurocentric relationships to race and power by forcing a distorted black face onto the arguments. Never are the more Afrocentric portions of the piece repudiated, they are simply not relevant to how the argument was being applied in the debate under the coaches conception of how the piece functions, showing how by framing the function of the argument, a pedagogy is produced where a bias interpretations of material can be produced in the name of "advancing black scholarship." To accentuate just how far the pieces application in debate veered from its initial artistic performance, upon seeing

Williams perform the piece on YouTube a year later, my first thought was how good of an argument the piece would be in a debate, only to realize that my debaters *already* had use the piece in debate rounds under an intellectual framework so different from the artist's that the piece was unrecognizable to me.

This highlights the danger of white Eurocentric co-option of black scholarship, where often well-meaning white academics can distort the black intellectual tradition so deeply that it becomes unrecognizable to the black students designed to educate. This is not to say that debaters accepted the coaches framing of the pieces, often using them in debates in ways that would frustrate the coach. What is important to note is that the coach took pleasure in contorting arguments from the black intellectual tradition into a Eurocentric framework. He would often say things like "they [the opposing debaters and coaches] are too stupid to realize we're just making a Foucault argument", showing that he clearly felt he was outsmarting his opposition and turning pieces of black radical thought into "real scholarship." The coaches actions mirrored the white Eurocentric academies insidious process of producing "black scholarship" which quotes black theorists, artists, and historical figures (at this claims to be antiracist) uses them in the service not of commenting on material conditions of oppressed black people, but instead to advance personal theirs of individual black liberation was within a Eurocentric academic framework.

A further interrogation into the dynamics of Towson debate allows Ani's analysis of white liberalism seeking to revive Eurocentrism and White Supremacy rather than undermine to be seen. When the Towson debate head coach constructed a coaching staff for the team, he invited friends who had a track record of competitive success to join the coaching staff. These choices included a former coach for Georgetown University, a graduate student at Johns Hopkins University with a focus on applying postmodern philosophical scholarship to debate, and a recently graduate debater noted for his use of poetry and the French thinker Jean Baudrillard. That the head coach would select, for a team made exclusively of black debaters focusing on critical race theory, a coaching staff made entirely of privileged white men and intimate relationship white liberal academics and competitive success in the community is an example of him acting out the foundational logic of white Eurocentric liberalism and the Negrophilia/Negrophobia paradox. By recruiting new staff centered on competitive success and familiarity with the white liberal academic canon, the coach was able to justify his actions by claiming that seem seeking to bring "nothing but the best" for his debaters, and introduce his debaters to "the highest levels of scholarship". It is important to remember that this process involved many other equally qualified debaters of color were either not recruited or chose not to come because of the head coaches inability to convince him that he would produce an environment conducive to their success. His pedagogical choices of focusing on

Eurocentric canon thus becomes a Negrophilic "civilizing mission" as the coach sought to bring intellectual "enlightenment" to his black debaters by centering his curriculum on the white liberal academic canon. Thus, the fundamental ethos of the team was not the empowerment of his debaters, but using black debaters as the raw material to prove the superiority of himself in particular as a coach and the white liberal academic traditional in general.

He framed his act explicitly as a corrective to the threat of black scholarship corrupting and hamstrings his debaters (i.e. limiting their intellectual "freedom"). This Negrophobic impulse extended not only to black scholarship but also black people as black mentors and black alumni of the program were seen as resources to be strategically utilize (as part time mentors, van drivers, and unpaid research assistants, and recruiters of high school debaters for the Towson team) but not given any power over the fundamental decision of the team or the allocation of team resources. In one particularly vivid example of this, the coach attempted to recruit and members of LBS as "headhunters", recruiting debaters from other schools to transfer to Towson for debate despite debate community rules against attempts to "poach" debaters from the competition, seeing that since members of LBS for volunteering their time and efforts for Towson debate, they will be exempt from these rules as they were actually employed by the team. This harkens back to the quote from Frank Wilderson; in both the Negrophilic and Negro phobic framework, the black is seen as subhuman, a resource to be exploded and utilized to serve white interests.

Exporting White Liberalism Racism: From the Academy to the Community

The material implications of the negrophilia/ negrophobia paradox can be seen in the context of political framing used by white liberals in Baltimore. For example, an argument LBS has continuously made is sad to tax money should be spent wisely by the Baltimore city government, with less focused on policing it will focus on investing in preventative programming done by community members. This deviates from the standard "white liberal" framing, which is Baltimore's problems, human overinvestment in downtown, tourist-centered areas of the city, and thus ignores the demands of homeowners in community outside of downtown. In the documentary "Fleeing Baltimore" placed on YouTube by a Baltimore Community association, this negrophilia/negrophobia paradox can be seen in visual terms, with white homeowners declaring the need to increase police presence to stop "bad" black criminals, visual represented on screen, in the name of protecting not only themselves, but also "good" black homeowners who otherwise would leave and move to the county without increased police presence, and "innocent" bystanders. The concerns of Black homeowners are collapsed into those of whites; a tool the documentarians used to inoculate themselves from criticism, saying that "black flight" was problem too.

To claim that the reality of middle class "black flight" proves that "white flight" was not radicalized ignores years of empirical data showing even with similar amenities, whites chose to leave neighborhoods when blacks move in in favor of racially homogenous neighborhoods, and property value correlates the race more closely than neighborhood quality. Black flight, typically occurring after white flight, could thus be seen as Black parents simply ̇ predicting they will get less services in majority Black neighborhoods and attempting to get access to better funded suburban schools because markets will reflect white flight in their property value. This is specifically race *conscious* thinking, in fact it's recognizing the reality of white supremacy and seeking to position Black families to survive in it, but it is narrated within the documentary as if it is color blind, liberal thinking "middle class Blacks want good neighborhoods too!" "They want police too!", showing how epistemic convergence serves to disarticulate the reality of Black thought into a form that is productive for white concerns, again showing the reality of interest convergence. In the video, these families are largely spoken for, again centering concerns on white liberal interests and using black bodies as tools to further those interests.

Watching the video, it is important to reflect on what Wilderson calls "the grammar of suffering"; homeowners lack the "freedom" to have their property

84

appreciate in value and to enjoy their community without violence. This reflects a Eurocentric liberalism that viewers on the previous analysis of John Locke, issuing alternative framings of "freedom" that would come from talking with different elements of the black community, for may seek the "freedom" to not be harassed by police, the "freedom" to have culturally competent services funding in their community, and the "freedom" that comes when white homeowners in a community realize that the wealth they have accumulated, and seek to further accumulate, originated in the enslavement and forced labor of black people. The documentary by the Community Association again frames black people as the essential threat; a negrophobic framing justified in the name of ostensibly helping black people, but is again revealed as merely "interest convergence." Race neutral "community investment" produces racialized result; as a quote "objective" evaluation of the market would reveal that the programs most likely to keep residents in the city, the most desirable programs, are those which reflect culture of those who have money. Thus, the city holds "colorblind" calls for projects, and disproportionately choices to Baltimore invest in white nonprofits, such as community theaters, music spaces, artist cooperatives, and community gardens, within the framework of urban development, and assuming that, if black people had good project, they should win in these open competitions. This is a paradigmatic example of what Charles Mills calls radicalized liberalism; as the city of Baltimore has rejected calls for increased minority hiring, and targeting of funding towards African-American projects, as that would be "unfair" to white people in the community, thus naturalizing the historical power differentials between white and black and reinforcing notions that white culture is preferable to black culture, and white organizations are more trustworthy and organized than black organizations. One administrator of State Grant money relayed to us that when it gives money for the arts, while Baltimore is over 60% Black, close to 90% of grant money for art programs would go to white artists, showing how the abstract, color-blind notion of "community improvement" in practice mean white control over communities, and while this does not always mean the complete exclusion of blacks from community (i.e. Negrophobia), it does close of a notion of Black community control and create a tacit demand that, in order to get resources, Blacks must adopt framings and performances acceptable/desirable to Whites (Negrophilia). In either framework, however, the dehumanization of Black bodies is present.

This racialized power dynamic has impacted LBS specifically. In our discussions of shifting the educational reform agenda away from merely focusing on more investment and better buildings, and towards comprehensive curriculum reform to include culturally competent black/African scholarship, LBS with typically met with the white global response that such calls were "not pragmatic", and that since the majority of opportunities in the city required mastery, which really meant identity, the white/Eurocentric culture.

A closer examination of this argument reveals several interesting tacit assumptions the steam from the arguments Eurocentric foundations. It assumes a pedagogy incorporating African centered/black scholarship to be mutually exclusive, or even specifically defined against, any discussions of the topics discussed within the traditional/Eurocentric framework. In our conversations, LBS would typically hear statements such as "black people need to learn science," "black people need to learn math," and "black people need to learn about things besides black people." Moreover, a common concern was students being "forced" into limited conceptions of Blackness, a fear reflecting white liberal concerns about individual freedom. Again, it is in the name of protecting Black student (negrophilia) that white liberal advocacy challenges/ demonizes a black education framework, and thus by extension those who teach from it (negrophobia). These shows an inability to conceptualize believe that Black/ African centered scholarship as a system of thought that can be applied to any topic, but instead assume it to be a static, essentialist system of beliefs focus on rejecting perceived whiteness and inculcating self-righteous individualism. In response to this, I would often give the example of the difference between teaching black students molecular science in the abstract, with pictures of molecules bonding and separating the focus of the lesson, and teaching black students molecular science within a black/African centered framework, focusing on the material implications for black students stemming from molecular science, such as the disproportionate rates of asthma emboli communities stemming from chemical reactions between car exhaust and sunlight, and reflecting a legacy of environmental racism. While the former operates the Universalists, colorblind abstraction, what with in all likelihood lead to students to think out the lesson, the latter focuses on relating the content of the lesson the lives of the students, designed to produce an attachment to the subject material that facilitates learning. Upon hearing this example, many of the white liberal critics of our curriculum/pedagogy, which failed to produce a response, as they had never conceptualize black/African centered scholarship as being able to be applied to "hard science". This example to the previous discussion of the academy, this inability to see black/African centered scholarship has a legitimate framework for thought must be seen at an extension of the superficial and Eurocentric academic caricaturists of black/African centered sought that had been circulated in the academy.

Similarly, a common concern often advanced by white liberals is that Black/African centered scholarship can't be a foundation for teaching because it represents a patriarchal/ hyper- masculine/ homophobia framework of Black Nationalism that limits the student's ability to conceptualize themselves as free, independent individuals. Again, when confront with the reality that many African tribes we're not patriarchal, but matriarchal, and that the shift to patriarchy was often promulgated by colonial power to consolidate their rule, white liberals often had no response, as their analysis had been based upon the academic caricature of black nationalist scholarship. Similarly, when we would explain that a Black/African centered framework would inject a discussion of structural white supremacy, and thus affirm same sex love because in a world of white supremacy, the ability to genuinely love produces the possibilities to fight systemic oppression in the name of a beloved community, white liberal commenters would often look puzzled, as love for them was not seen in the context of a community, but strictly as a space for individuals to experience personal freedom. By viewing the connections between the debate community, the Academy, and the community, we can see how white supremacy produces a vicious cycle; Eurocentric/white ideas are taken to be the norm, and thus are taught in the academy. People use the knowledge they get from the Academy to make life decisions and to contextualize their politics, which then shifts material resources to Eurocentric thinkers and centralize power with some white/Eurocentric organizations, which means the next generation of students are students are taught that the most practical/best education they should seek out in school is knowledge about Eurocentric/white institutions.

In both instances, the assumption is that the traditional curriculums silence on issues of race made it "race natural". This is the only framework where concerns about forced assimilation into specific view about identity make sense. By staying silent on race, the traditional academic curriculum sends powerful racist messages to Black and Brown youth too numerous to list here. The teaching of Eurocentric text, the exclusion of Black/African authors, the omission of discussions of slavery and American imperial conquests, all teach youth their culture is either secondary, redundant (since everything happened in Europe first) or irrelevant, and tacitly instructs youth that violence against their ancestors was a "necessary evil" to construct the "great nation" we have today. That the ire of white liberal would be directed at us for attempting to inject culture assumes that in the current environment we are at a balance in terms of cultural conversations (one that our Black/African Centered approach would disrupt). In reality, the current curriculum is so *radically* Eurocentric and reflect such deep notions of European intellectual superiority, that only a targeted, intentional insertion of cultural and critical analysis can even begin to move things back towards what could be called "balance". This reflects Mills' discussion of the necessity to adopt seeming "anti-liberal" measure, like reparations, in order to correct for years of injective as the only way to have a genuinely "liberal" moral/political order. Far from radical, our measure simple sought an intellectual middle ground, a fact to which liberal were often blinded by their Eurocentric liberals and their framing of us with the negrophilia/negrophobia paradox.

From the Micro to the Macro:
Liberal Academic Negrophilia/Negrophobia as an Institution

A story comparing an LBS venture with a venture spear -headed by the aforementioned Towson Debate coach may help to clarify the importance of thinking of Eurocentric academy's Negrophilic/Negrophobia relationship to blackness in terms of macro-level institution rather than just micro level interpersonal/individual relationships. Over the summer months, it's common for high school debaters to attend debate summer camps taught by college debate coaches and college debaters. Ironically, both the Towson debate coach question and Leaders of a Beautiful Struggle were holding debate summer camp for high school students in Baltimore at the same time. While the Towson camp focused more on postmodern theory in relationship to politics and power (while incorporating Black teachers and Towson debaters), the LBS debate camp was explicitly focused on centering on scholarship and the black radical tradition in teaching debaters from urban debate league from the country how to apply the scholarship in the high school debates. By this time the behavior of the Towson debate coach, including verbal harassment and physical intimidation, had already strained relationship between the coach and the debaters on the squad. Also, I was clear that as a coach I would likely not have my contract renewed and thus would not be employed by Towson University debate for the next school year.

91

These tensions boiled over when two of the Towson University debaters, who while being contractually obligated to work as a Towson University campus of the scholarships but were generally underutilized and not given specific daily tasks as a Towson coach came to the LBS debate camp to do an exhibition debate for the use at the camp. While the coach had voiced support for the efforts of LBS is holding a debate camp, he took extreme offense at the Towson University debaters leaving the Towson camp to do an event at the LBS camp. He claimed that the acts showed the debaters to not be committed to their responsibilities, potentially in breach of their scholarship contracts, and generally insubordinate and proceeded to threaten to take away scholarship money from the Towson University debaters.

It is beyond the scope of this project to recount in detail all the events that would follow. Members of LBS, as alumni of the program and mentors/advocates for the Towson University's debaters, would go on to meet with the head coach, his wife (the director of debate for Towson University), administrators within the Towson Communication's Department, and other high-ranking Towson officials. Eventually, after filing a threat incident report detailing the coach's numerous examples of inappropriate behavior, the coach was removed from his position. However, the Towson University director debate, while in formally sequestering herself away from the debaters, still had control over the teams budget and, using similar logic to her husband, would rule the debaters desire to attend the Harvard University debate tournament as selfish and misplaced and therefore refused to sanction the students traveled to this tournament, despite a long tradition of the team funding the trip and the students themselves raising the money to attend the tournament themselves to online crowd funding efforts. LBS again intervened on the student's behalf, posting an article the Leaders of a Beautiful Struggle website alerting the public to the behavior of the dismissed head coach, and questioning the logic of the director of the debate for Towson University of not allowing the students, who had proven themselves to be among the best debaters in America only two weeks prior at the Kentucky University debate tournament, to not attend one of the most important and prestigious debate tournaments in the country because of perceived insubordination. Eventually, through the efforts of LBS as well as Towson University Black alumni and concerned members of the debate community, the students were allowed to compete at the Harvard University debate tournament, and would go on, despite not having a Towson University coaching staff in Baltimore but relying on the efforts of volunteer coaching from graduate students at the University of Pittsburgh, to win the 2014 Cross-Examination Debate Association (CEDA) college debate national championship.

Here the previous discussion of psychology becomes applicable, as in this example we began to see how abstract concepts like the emotional dynamics (or rather it is referred to in some literature as "affective dynamics") of white liberalism can have very real, material implications for black bodies. The frustration the Towson debate coach felt and seeing two of his students leave "his" debate camp to volunteer at the LBS debate camp is, in many ways, objectively illogical. By competing in exhibition debate, the students would receive valuable experience that could help them achieve success in the upcoming debate season, and given the verbally stated support for the efforts of LBS (LBS members served key roles in coach members of the Towson debate team the previous season), and given that the students limited responsibilities for the Towson debate camp occurred predominately at night (the students were serving as Residential Assistants), it is hard to find a material reason why this act would warrant such a disproportionately intense response. When this response, however, is evaluated through the lens of white liberalism's Negrophlia/Negrophobia paradox, a logical pattern can be discerned. By hosting a debate camp, the Towson debate coach saw himself as coach for academic play that mirrors liberalism's foundational logic of abstract, individualistic freedom. While the Towson camp incorporated discussions of race and racism through the contributions of the minority faculty and the Towson debate students of the coach, these contributions towards collective empowerment for oppressed people were not the foundational concern of the camp. Rather, they were just another set of tools to be deployed in the service of competitive academic freedom. This can be seen through the Towson debate camp incorporation of arguments such as "patriarchy is good because it allows for stronger national security" in response to feminist critiques of patriarchy, which were allowed as they were seen as legitimate extension of "academic freedom." It also gives framework to understand why the coach was so enthusiastic to embrace *certain* forms of critical race scholarship, the forms that focused more on artistic performance and "radical freedom" and egoistic intellectual competition.

This is in fundamental distinction to the pedagogy of the LBS debate camp. While the Towson debate camp used postmodern theorists such as Michel Foucault and Giles Deleuze as their "symbols", the LBS debate camp was called the Eddie Conway liberation Institute in name of wrongfully imprisoned former Baltimore Black Panther Eddie Conway. While the Towson debate camp prided itself on spending hours and hours on research, and for its unique rituals such as late-night moon gazing, the LBS debate incorporated traveling into the Baltimore community to visit cultural sites, to see artistic performances, the eat at local Black owned restaurants, and generally connected to the community at foundational to pedagogy of the camp. While the Towson debate camp prided itself on its highly qualified guest speakers (including the recently crowed national champion from Georgetown), LBS debate camp eschewed as much as possible the lecture format, preparing exhibition debates, artistic performances, humanity conversations, and an all hands on experience which placed the students as drivers of the campus pedagogy, rather than the recipient of elite knowledge. Of these points substantiate the Eurocentric/African centered distinction made by on the; while the Towson camp was designed to produce elite academic games players, the LBS camp was designed first and foremost to promote a community consciousness design to help the students use debating as a tool for communal empowerment. It's interesting, therefore, that the Towson debate coach would evaluate the Towson debater's desire to volunteer at the LBS debate camp at having a zero-sum trade-off with that commitment to the Towson debate camp. Rather than recognizing that because of the distinct pedagogical foundations of the two camps, a very different type of "affective" work is being done at the LBS camp, design to produce into communal bonds between black people to help them survive and resist the conditions of white supremacy, the Towson debate coach evaluates this desire to help the LBS camp within his Eurocentric framework of individualism, claiming the students to be "selfish" and "not committed to the group cause" when in actuality their action show the exact *opposite* orientation. His frustration thus should be seen as reflecting a sense of personal rejection. Within this framework this can be seen quite literally as "why don't you want to play with me?"

Here is useful to refer back to Franz Fanon and his quote book *Black Skin, White Mask* who quoted Bernard Wolfe in saying that "the smile of the 'Black Man' always means a gift". With this statement than on his arguing that within the white communal imagination, whites often seek validation and reassurance from Blacks (the smile), and this affirms their sense of superiority; after all, if Black people like them, they must be doing something good, right? The long legacy of racist caricatures of smiling Black people, and the enduring historical tropes of the happy, dancing black man (Sambo) and the loving, maternal black nanny (Mammy) support this idea that whites desire performances of Blacks that assuage white fears of black anger and support notions that blacks are thankful for white protection and help. The debate coach has the power to turn his desire for affirming black performances into a demand, as he can use the possibility of the deniable scholarship money to coerce these performances from his debaters. Similarly, the coach has to power, in the case of assistance coaches, to literally make these affirming performances a job requirement, with the coach telling me I would not be hired back if I did not "make it more clear to the boss (his wife) that you liked her." Within the political economy of white liberalism, this desire for affirmation from black bodies can become a demand of acquiescence from black bodies, it is here that seemingly altruistic white liberalism, when seen within the Negrophilia/Negrophobia paradox, can become a violent force in furthering the logic of white supremacy and the institutional power powerlessness of blacks in favor of centralizing institutional power with white institutions.

This is also a textbook example of the distinction between bias and racism. While it could be argued, and in fact it was by some, that the LBS debate camps explicit focus on black communal empowerment and black

97

scholarship was "bias" against white people in white scholarship. However, since no one at the LBS debate camp, despite a bevy of academic, community, and debate accomplishments, had institutional control over things like scholarships, travel budgets, or hiring decisions for the University, they had no ability to turn that supposed bias into material discrimination. The exact opposite was true with Towson, where the head coach, a notoriously egocentric and brash personality who had already once been fired from Towson Debate by a previous administration, was able to rise through the ranks to a point where he had institutional power over Black debaters after several other more highly qualified Black and Brown candidates had been denied his position in the past.

Reflexive Black Institution Building as Corrective for Liberal White Supremacy

It is by design this paper concludes with a discussion of institutional power. As I hope this paper would help explain, too often those who seek to advance progressive antiracist praxis frame that resistance in the context of individual action (language choice, "consciousness-raising", etc). Within the framework of the argument I have laid out, to the reflection of the Eurocentric foundations of liberal political sought, focusing on catharsis and all atonement by individual rather than addressing collective/ institutional solutions. This is not to say that individual action and reflection has no place in the revolutionary struggle. On the contrary, has argued in this paper, is only through embracing the need for material action will collective empowerment that the individual against experiences in context necessary for successful reflection. Moreover, solutions for the problem of racism what supremacy are traditionally frame within the context of democratizing or even radicalizing existing institutions. However, this paper raises serious doubts about such strategies, as given the insidious nature of liberal white supremacy, the Academy and the negrophilia/negrophobia paradox, even well-meaning attempts to correct the legacy contemporary of racism/white supremacy can be contorted, processed within the Eurocentric liberal framework, and used to further the interests of the status quo through "interest convergence." Thus, a framework of "Reflexive Black Institution Building" is presented as a strategy to frame strategies of empowerment. It takes the limitation of white liberalism seriously, arguing that blacks must develop spaces that do not depend on the patronage and support of whites for their survival, but instead are supported by, and thus have fidelity to, the black community. This stems not from an ideological resistance to whiteness, but out of a "prophetic" pragmatism which argues its simple logical that given the history of America and an objective analysis of Eurocentric/White culture, blacks will always be subject to damaging "interest convergence" if their notions of political uplift are entirely dependent on access to or reform of dominate structures, and thus blacks must supplement their relationship with these structures with structures produce by and for themselves.

An examination of the Eddie Conway liberation Institute (ECLI) helps to clarify what is meant by the phrase "reflexive Black institution building" and helps conceptualize concerns and criticisms of the framing. For years, members of LBS had attended or taught at a number of regional and national debate institutes hosted by predominately white institutions, which reflected the pedagogy of the traditional/white liberal debate community. After realizing that years of black debaters having high-level success in high school and college debate had produced a critical mass of potential camp instructors and high school students interested in learning about applying critical race theory to debate, the ECLI was envisioned as a three week summer debate camp run by black debaters/ coaches at a Historically Black College/University. This was seen as serving multiple objectives.

First, it would serve as a space where race conscious high school debaters, who often have little to no coaching and direction of their arguments, could learn from college debaters and college coaches who had in depth experience applying this literature base to debate, allowing them to not only have connections to mentors facilitate that gross as debaters and their potential much regulation to college, but also allow them to theorize the relationship to critical race theory outside of dominations of interest convergence and Eurocentric co-option of critical race theory, which have become prevalent in many high school debaters application and utilization of race in debate. Thus goal was to begin to shift the standard for what the debate community considers a good "race debater" away from what we saw as increasingly dangerous benchmarks of "whoever could make an argument about race sounds almost like a traditional postmodern debate critique argument" or "with most effective at mobilizing the white guilt of the judges to win debates" and toward metrics that valued fidelity to the tradition of critical race theory and its focus on using academic analysis to reflect and bolster material community empowerment. While abstract notions of freedom to not necessarily hold a central place in his framework (and as such it differs from the Eurocentric liberal framework), an analysis the address the concern that a focus on "Black" institution building somehow limits the freedom of adopters into some essentialized notion of blackness, for in the context of the ECLI, it was a desire to deal with the tacit limitations of Eurocentric critical race theory that informed the camps pedagogy. Far from being a space of free play that this Black institution building would assume, if students were limited to forms of race argumentation that fit the preconceived notions of their judges, typical 18-25 years old white college students or young teacher/coaches, then forms of expression are de facto limited to those which "converge" with the preconceived notions of their coaches and judges.

An example of what this mean in practice comes from two young women who attended the camp. Their argument included an argument about reclaiming the black female body through artistic performance, in this case dance. This is very similar to the argument the Towson debate coached presented to some of his debaters in his time at Towson, an argument which the framed through the lens of "radical freedom" from perceived limitations of Blackness and femininity being a politically useful tool, as it resisted in use of identity categories that were critical tools used by people and governments to do violence to people. While the argument citied Black feminist theorists, the core logic of the argument came from white performance theorists argue that identify categories, in the abstract where used to control people and mark them as "others", and by resisting these identifications, it thus also forestalled the debaters to debate in way to claim a linage to a tradition of Black communal struggle or historical cultural relationships, such as African culture, as that would contradict the argument. At ECLI and throughout the year, the young women developed their argument into a critique of the white gaze of their judges claiming their dance was not for them, but against their attempt to limit and define their bodies, and that their dancing was in a lineage of African dance that helped situate them as Black women into a larger culture tradition that gave them the psychological and spiritual resources necessary to fight against a system of white supremacy. To an untrained eye, these two arguments look essentially the same (black women dance and talk about racism in debate) an interrogation of the foundational logic of the two arguments reveals essential differences. While the former depends on linking black performance with an liberal individualistic framework that seeks to create a link to the logic of their white judges, the latter challenges the judges and reorients scholarship toward a cultural connection in the name of action in the Black community. By pushing the argument outside of the limits of liberal/postmodern scholarship, the young women were not only able to explore facets of scholarship that were deemed irrelevant within a Eurocentric relationship to race scholarship (such as Africans history), but, ironically, able to have a strategic advantage over their opponents, whose ignorance about the Black community and African history meant they were less equipped to response to these arguments then for arguments that situate race within a more comfortable "postmodern/ liberal" framework. This shows a "pragmatic" and "reflective" vision allows for Black institution building to go beyond preconceived limitation of this framework. Far from the caricaturized vision of Black nationalism (where ECLI would in theory have instructed the girls to not dance in front of white men) the camp sought to give the girls the cultural and psychological framework necessary to help the girls be the agents of their debate rather than the subject of fetishized and co-opted by their white judges, and in the process help strategically tweak it in a results oriented fashion to help promote the successes of the argument.

Further clarity on the logic of Reflexive Black Institution Building comes from interrogating the other major goals for ECLI. The camp was envisioned as pieces in a larger framework for LBS the use of debate to foster

Black leadership and opportunity in the city of Baltimore. By hosting a high level national debate summer camp at a Historically Black College, this helped produce a pool of well-trained recruits for a potential college debate team at this school. By having an elite debate camp on campus, the camp would help to challenge the narrative that HBCUs are less rigorous or desirable in comparison with historically white schools, and thus help garner support for the team by recruiting high level debaters, who are often attractive students for universities. Once on campus, the debaters would serves as member of Leaders of a Beautiful Struggle, using their experience in debate to get academic theory to inform their community activism, and using their activism to get the lived experience to help inform their arguments in debate. This virtuous cycle would lead to successful student debaters who would go on to establish connections in the community, allowing them to matriculate to working in the community or the academy with a trainings in how to orient their professional work toward communal empowerment. Moreover, independent of any debater team at a HBCU or ventures related to LBS, the camp was designed to serve as a communal gather place for what has become a diaspora of Black debaters/coaches, providing not only in a material sense an opportunity for summer employment, but also an opportunity for Black community building outside of the white intuitional gaze.

This shows the logic of Reflexive Black Institution Building as having a material intuitional focus that helps show in practice the concept of "prophetic pragmatism." In response to the argument that Black Institution Building romanticizes Black institutions (like HBCUs) the camp realizes that an HBCU would need a material reason to support a debate team and the camp seeks to provide this by offering the possibility of recruiting high achieving students to the HBCU through debate, as well as offering the possibility of national level debate success (and the attended positive public relations). Far from romanticizing black institutions, this concept reflects on the reality of interest convergence, but seeks to strategic find interests between blacks rather than accepting the limitations that come with finding ways to converge with the interests of whites. Not all interests converge equally, so while the Black Institution Building concept would reject the logic traditional notions of pragmatism, it seeks to redefine pragmatism within a Black prophetic tradition that seeks to create virtuous cycle of empower between different facets of the Black community.

Conclusion: Not a Perversion, but a Paradigm

I wanted to conclude this paper by reflecting on my experience with Towson debate, specifically my portrayal of the actions of the head coach that have been the dominant framework for this paper. In my experience discussing issues of racism and white supremacy, there is a specific catch 22 when it comes to how one frames an argument. If we speak in the abstract about larger theories of power, people comment that the theory is too speculative and demand specific examples. Conversely, where I frame my analysis through specific instance and people as example, critics tend to dismiss the critiques as "personal differences" and assuming the instance is isolated and not representing a larger political problem. This is why I have chosen to link a specific person experience to a larger political paradigm. I'm sure some will still dismiss the stores presented as action of individual "bad white allies." Though the circumstances presented here are no doubt complex, the desire to round down this structural criticism to the lens of individual failings proves my critique of the individualist framework for white liberalism seeking to save Eurocentric thought from its excesses. While it is easy to think that a more considerate, reflexive approach would allow for a better relationship between the coach and the debaters (and I do not doubt this is true), the argument here is that the actions of the coach are not about individual biases, but an intellectual paradigm of Eurocentric liberal thought. Contrary to what the reader might conclude by my statements, I would not necessary conclude that the former coach is a "bad person," in fact I do believe that the coach honestly felt his action were what were best for his students. What I am arguing, however, is that his actions are not a perversion of the white liberal paradigm, but merely revealing its foundational logic in the context a specific institutional setting. As examples from non-debate academy and community activism show, the actions that led to such intense antagonism on the Towson team are merely reflections of a larger system of Eurocentric liberal thought that is exported by the Eurocentric academy into the community. By defining the problem, the Eurocentric academy has incredible power in society, in that it defines the scope of conceivable solutions and promotes a specific framework (an ahistorical notion of individual freedom) by which ethical thought and action are evaluated. In this framework, the Towson debate coach is not fundamentally different from most white liberal non-profit workers and academics; he merely made the mistake of saying openly what many people think privately. The theory the negrophilia/negrophobia paradox and liberal white supremacy takes the explanation for what happen on the Towson squad *outside* of the framework of personal failing, and into the framework of a manifestation of larger white supremacist culture.

In the face of its Eurocentric cultural reality, I present Reflexive Black Institution Building to reframe what is often seen as an individualistic conversation into an institutional conversation. It seeks to take seriously the concerns of those who question identity based organizing (such as those who worry about these action serving the purposes of Black capitalism or being co-opted by liberal multiculturalism) by injecting the modifier "reflexive" before black institution building. This raises the question of what exactly is being reflected upon. A Reflective Black Institution Building framework would reflect on the past failure of Black Institution Building Efforts, including its shortcomings relating to gender and sexual orientation, as well as the under reported and under theorized successes stories. It would also reflect on the Black experience in America using Frank Wilderson's framework of "Afropessimism" as a framework. An analysis of the negrophilia/negrophobia paradox prevents this framework from smoothly functioning with into liberal multicultural framework, as a historical interrogation of "interest convergence" would see that seductive opportunities to ingratiated into multicultural liberalism often serve the dominate interests and tacitly limit the scope of potential solutions to Black oppression.

By challenging the white affective framework for liberal politics, it seeks to put Wilderson's academic theory to work, using it as a compass to navigate the pitfalls of advocating Black Institution Building in a world of liberal white supremacy. This addresses one of the more overarching concerns about Wilderson's theory, that his views of blackness being in an "antagonistic" relationship to the white world limits possibilities for agency and action. I would hope by now the reader would have a skepticism of these concerns about agency, as again these reflects a Eurocentric notions of Black scholars being dangerous for limiting the freedom for blacks. Far from limiting resistance, this reflective view empowers resistance by presenting an empirical framework where pervious opaque political dynamics of white liberalism and liberal white supremacy become clear. In light of its pessimistic view of the ability for the reality of Black liberation in the dominate white liberal framework, an analysis of this academic theory has led us at Leaders of a Beautiful Struggle to material advocate for autonomous, reflective Black led and Black controlled intuitions, a realization that should be viewed as a *hopeful* concussion to a pessimistic reality of contemporary Black life in America. Ani's theory provides meat to the skeleton Wilderson lays out, giving a cultural foundation for the observations of Wilderson's theory. By laying out a cultural paradigm for European thought, actors can engage politics with a framework for politics that is not only descriptive, but can be predictive of white liberal opposition to race conscious political organizing. In my personal experience, without this framework, activist often interpret this resistance as personal attacks by people they thought were allies or friends. This framework address the serious issue of the affective entanglement, arguing not that productive affective engagements/ coalitions across race are impossible, but merely given the history of racism/ white supremacy and the culture of Eurocentric liberals, blacks in America simply cannot depend on the benevolence of white institutions for the liberation of survival.

Given the material reality of white supremacy, the states at play in the academic engagements with blackness are nothing less than the survival of the Black community, but unfortunately this view is generally not shared within the liberal academy. It is typically seen as a safe space for exploration and play for young students. This paper challenges readers to take the need for institutional change seriously. What students are taught (and not taught) has serious implications for politics, and this paper hopes to present the importance of institutional engagement. While the story of Towson Debate may seem extreme for some, it will seem unnervingly familiar for others, as black students all over the country have been commenting on the reality of Liberal Academic racism. The Negrophilia/Negrophobia paradox gives a framework for interpreting this experience that can be applied to larger structures of politics, and it is in the spirit of the tradition of critical race theory that I call for concerned readers in the academy to use the lessons of this text of strategize structural change in their institutions. This is distinct from the logic of protest or critique, actions that while seeming often to be radical can in the abstract fall back into a logic of individual freedom and *remove* injustice rather than producing positive institutions to protect the material interests for oppressed people. It is hoped that the examples presented in this chapter serve as guidance, but I would caution against seeing them as a template. In the tradition of (prophetic) pragmatism, solutions should reflect the conditions and positions of actions, rather than having fidelity to any abstract or romanticized examples of resistance. What is important is that readers theorize ways to affirm the hope of classic critical race theorists such as Derrick Bell; those who have access to the academy view the academy as a tool to empower the forgotten masses within the Black community.

The Non-Profit Industrial Complex in Baltimore

By Dayvon Love

The non-profit industrial complex is a phenomenon that is
at least as dangerous to livelihood of Black people as the
prison industrial complex. It has been an impediment to
the development of indigenous, community based Black
Leadership on important issues. This has allowed white
people to use our bodies and ideas to prop up and support
white institutional power. Here in Baltimore, the non-profit
industry and foundations drive much of the dialogue and
political advocacy around issues that face Black people.
This is a concept that many people will find very troubling
because it implicates the work of a lot of well meaning
white people who have dedicated their lives to helping the
"disadvantaged." One of my mentors, John Morris, who is
the dean of the school of Urban Planning at Sojourner
Douglass College, once explained to me that there are three
elements to the white liberal imagination. There is the poor
helpless Negro, the special Negro, and the white Savior.
The poor helpless Negros are the Black people who are in
need of saving.   These are the people that non-profit
organizations purport to want to save from their misery.
They are helpless because they do not possess the ability to
help themselves. The special Negro is the Black person
who was miraculously able to become equal to white
people.   They are special because they are not like the

others who are inherently unable to improve their own lives. The white Savior is the notion that white people are indispensable to the collective empowerment of Black people. This idea is what helps to drive the non-profit industrial complex. All of this is based on the idea of Black inferiority.

The notion of Black inferiority is embedded deep in the American psyche. It transcends political ideology, profession, personality and intellect. The notion of Black inferiority actively contributes to what we call the non-profit industrial complex. We borrowed this term from an organization of feminists of color called INCITE!, in a book called *The Revolution Will Not Be Funded: Beyond the Non-Profit Industrial Complex*. They define this phenomenon as "a system of relationships between government, the owning classes, foundations, and nonprofit social service and social justice organizations that results in the surveillance, control, derailment, and everyday management of political movements." In order for this industry to function it requires that Black inferiority be the framework for interpreting the lives, issues and needs of Black people. The reduction of Black people's lives to mere objects that can be managed by institutions in this industry is made possible by the deep-seeded notion of Black inferiority. To understand how deep it penetrates the American collective consciousness we have to develop an understanding of the way that Black inferiority structures all of modern civil society. It is literally the building block that undergirds the internal logic of civil society.

The project of modernity and the rise of Europe were intimately linked to colonialism and European domination of the world. In order for Europe to justify is domination of the world it had to produce historical narratives about themselves and others that would rationalize the exploitation of people of color around the world. The enslavement of Africans could only be effective if there was an effective campaign to remove Africans out of the respectful commentary of human history. All of the "Enlightenment" and modernity was predicated on the assertion that Africa had no culture worth studying. Georg Wilhelm Friedrich Hegel, who is foundational to modern philosophy, once said in his book *The Philosophy of History* that

> "Egypt will be considered in reference to the passage of the human mind from its Eastern to its Western phase, but it does not belong to the African Spirit. What we properly understand by Africa, is the Unhistorical, Undeveloped Spirit, still involved in the conditions of mere nature, and which had to be presented here only as on the threshold of the World's History."

Ivan Van Sertima, one of the finest scholars on Ancient African History, once remarks that Egyptology was an academic discipline developed during the Renaissance, was created for the purposes of theorizing Egypt out of Africa and disconnecting it from its Southern Nile Valley roots in order to continue to propagate the myth of Africa being a primitive people with no history. When scholars and educators teach students about ancient civilizations they often start with Greece but fail to mention the great ancient African civilizations that taught the ancient world much of what it knew about science, art, technology etc, this contributes to the myth of Black inferiority. By representing Ancient Egyptians as "middle eastern" instead of showing them as the dark complected descendents of Ethiopians and Nubians it allows the societal notion that Africans, who today would be described as Black, are not responsible for the development of great and advanced civilizations. Omitting the greatness of Ancient African civilizations makes it easier to create a history in which it seems rational that Africans were enslaved and that Africa had been colonized by Europeans. The failure to mention that many of the ancient Greek gods were African (Athena was the goddess of wisdom, for example), the first steel was smelted in what we call Tanzania today, or that in Kemet (what we call Egypt today) practitioners of medicine were doing surgery using anesthetics, and many other things of that sort, sends the subliminal message that Africans are an inferior people. Scholars like Dr. John Henrik Clarke, John G. Jackson, Asa Hilliard, Marimba Ani, Cheikh Anta Diop and many others have provided us with the scholarly resources to know with scientific certainty and validity that ancient African civilizations were far more advanced and sophisticated than many of us can imagine. Even those of us who proclaim to be advocates for Black people carry with us notions of the inherit inferiority of Africans. Even I carried this notion well into the stage where I became knowledgeable about white supremacy and racism.

I was once having a conversation with a gentleman named Jerrel Baker. He was coaching a debate team at a public school in Baltimore several years ago. He is a learned scholar on African history and he told me about a book called "They Came Before Columbus" by Ivan Van Sertima. He told me that the thesis of the book was that Africans had been to the Americas long before Europeans had come. I didn't say this out loud, but my internal response to this was, "why do we have to say that we were the first to come to America? We don't need to prove this to be true in order to substantiate that we live in a white supremacist society. We have all the data that we need, why put out such a conspiracy theory and undermine the credibility of the work that all of us are trying to do?" I dismissed it as just a thought experiment that I had come to associate with conspiracy theorists bent on claiming that we did everything Europeans did before they did it. A couple of years later I was surfing YouTube for lectures to listen to and I came across Ivan Van Sertima's lecture on They Came Before Columbus. I listened to it and was blown away. After I listened to it I went and got Van Sertima's book. After listening to the lecture and reading the book I discovered two things. First, that Africans actually were in the western hemisphere before Europeans even knew that there was a western hemisphere, the evidence is just overwhelming. But more importantly I realized why I was so quick to dismiss the idea. What I really thought but didn't realize was "Africans couldn't have built ships and navigated the ocean." My dismissal of the idea of Africans coming to the western hemisphere was predicated on the idea that African didn't have the capability of traveling the oceans. I knew this because the question I had to ask myself was, "why is it controversial that Africans came to American before Europeans?" The only substantive reason why it would be such a controversial thought is because the very notion of Black capability and capacity is controversial. Having had very little knowledge of the history of people of African descent in the ancient world it was easy for me to internalize the notion of African inferiority without even knowing it. This was a very important moment for me because it allowed me to see that even people who are educated and committed to the struggle for liberation of Black people can carry notions of Black inferiority that certainly have implications on how we organize politically.

The argument that I am making here is that all of us who are socialized in American culture are socialized to believe in Black inferiority, no matter how progressive or race-conscious we claim to be. Mainstream society very rarely circulates images or narratives of Black people demonstrating the capacity to effectively govern and operate large institutions. When people narrate the story of the Montgomery Bus Boycott of 1955 people often focus on Mrs. Rosa Parks's refusal to get off of the bus, but very little emphasis is put on the level of community organizing and political strategizing that was required to fight Jim Crow laws in Montgomery. Imagine all of the organizational capacity it took to organize an alternative transportation infrastructure that was good enough to replace the public transit system in Montgomery for several months. This demonstrates more administrative capacity than many city government agencies. Yet this is not reflected in the way that the Montgomery bus boycott is narrated. Most people don't even know that Mrs. Parks was a tremendous community organizer in her own right. That period in history is often represented as a moment of appeal to the sentiments of whites, instead of coordinated political actions. Even if we look at the work of Dr. Martin Luther King Jr, many people are familiar with his speeches, but not with his organizing work with the poor people's campaign. Many people don't even realize that he was the leader of an organization called the Southern Christian Leadership Conference that did organizing on the ground. His last organizing effort was to attempt to get decent wages for sanitation workers in Memphis Tennessee. This is the kind of organizing work that is not often talked about in mainstream political discourse. Notions of Black capacity and institution management are often omitted from our narratives of the history of people of African descent.

This is reinforced by the structural position that Black people are in that represent Black people as naturally occupying domestic positions. (Sidebar-I want to be very clear, I have a high respect for domestic work and in my commentary here am not all suggesting that domestic work is work for inferior people, but we live in a society that has relegated this kind of work to the status of a servant. This is the context from which I am describing domestic/service work, not that I think it is work for inferior people). For instance, I attended a predominately white university. I can imagine that even though many of the students may not be overtly bigoted, many of their professors where non-Black, where as many of the people who make up the custodial staff or the people serving food are Black. Even though there may be no conscious effort to assign Black people to designation of naturally being subservient to whites, this experience produced the subliminal message that this kind of work was more natural for Black people than for anyone else.

The notion of Black inferiority is deeply embedded in the minds of people all over this country, and is exported around the world. It is this notion that is the fulcrum for the non-profit industrial complex. Much of what is commonplace in the non-profit world are white people who have not immersed themselves in the history and culture of Black people thinking they can come into our communities and fix them. Take a moment to really think about how arrogant that is. People who know very little about the conditions that plague Black people, people who don't have any knowledge of the history of Black people think they are qualified to govern and operate institutions that are primarily populated by Black people. This is a manifestation of white supremacy that does not require ill intentions or malice toward Black people. It is the soft bigotry of white superiority that Americans are socialized to believe in without their active acknowledgement.

This is a phenomenon that would not be tolerated in other communities. Would groups devoted to the empowerment of women who are striving for gender equality allow men to run and operate the League of Women Voters? Would it make sense to anyone if the Korean Merchant Association allowed white people to chair their organization? Would Jewish people allow anyone who isn't Jewish to chair and govern AIPAC? I think I can say fairly confidently that most people would answer all the questions in the negative. So why does it make sense when people do this to Black people? The fundamental notion of Black inferiority is the only way we can explain why it would seem rational to anyone that white people from privileged communities could come into Black communities and have substantively positive impact on them without having immersed themselves in the history and culture of Black people. The entire enterprise of the non-profit industry relies on the notion of Black inferiority in order to justify foundations and philanthropic institutions financing the thought experiments of white folks that are then carried out on our people to advance their professional careers and livelihoods. According to Non-Profit Quarterly "eight percent of nonprofit board members are black, three percent are Hispanic, and an astonishing 30% of all nonprofit boards report that 100% of their members are white. As we have previously noted, the Council on Foundations survey found foundation boards to be roughly as white as nonprofit boards." The notion of Black inferiority has created a context where people generally can't imagine Black people having the capacity and capability to effectively operate an organization. We are often employees and mid-management of these organizations but are typically not given the executive leadership roles afforded to whites. This is a trend throughout the non-profit industry. According to The Chronicle of Philanthropy in 2009, 3.5% of the top 400 charities are run by Black people. We see this in Urban Debate League around the country. Urban Debate Leagues were started in the late 80's to help create access to policy debate to "inner city youth." George Soros and the Open Society gave millions of dollars primarily to white people who were interested in fostering debate in cities around the country. Baltimore is one of those cities. It has been approximately 20 years since the inception of Urban Debate Leagues around the country. There are now alumnae of these UDL's who have won national college debate championships, started grassroots organizations, have receive advanced degrees, become tenured professors and gone on to have professional careers. In spite of this, when we look around the country we still see that the national leadership of UDL's as well as the executive directors of many of the local UDL organizations are white people. This is just one manifestation of the way that the non-profit industrial complex protect white power and interest, even when they purport to want to empower Black people.

The structure of non-profits is particularly limiting. 501c3 status (which is the tax designation for non-profit organizations) has a stated purpose of helping to support entities that seek to improve the public good. Contributions to non-profits are tax deductible, which incentivize people to contribute to these organizations. The trade off is that these organizations cannot have explicit involvement in electoral politics. This arrangement makes sense for charitable organizations. But it begs the question of whether the people who are starting non-profits are interested in giving charity to Black people or seeking justice. These are two very different objectives. Anyone who claims to understand the condition of Black people should know that charity will not fix our problems. There is a need for social transformation that will require political and economic interventions and flexibility that the 501c3 status does not allow for. For instance, there may be public officials that need to be voted out of office, this requires resources and organizations. But non-profits are prohibited from engaging in that kind of activity. This means that non-profits are not structured to produce social transformation, but they are structured merely to provide charity to "needy" people. What is interesting about the notion of supporting organizations that seek to promote the public good is that the public good in a white supremacist society is probably not good for Black people. Black people typically live in social context that have drastically different social, economic, and political needs. The conditions that inspire people to come in to our communities and create non-profit organizations speak to the difference in the issues that we face. These issues require specific organizations that are committed to the welfare of Black people. This is not necessarily a "public good" that is made a policy consideration of civil society. Put differently there is no public outcry against institutional racism, which explains that lack of institutional structures in American social and political systems that are designed to address institutional racism. If you look at any of the literature, or website, or materials that describe the work of major foundations and non-profits that serve Black people in Baltimore, not one of them emphasize the importance independent Black institutions. This concept does not even appear once. You can look at the Open Society Institute, The Abell Foundation, The Baltimore Family League, the Safe and Sound Campaign, Baltimore Communities Foundation and many other organizations in Baltimore and you won't find these ideas even come up once. Here are some of the mission statements of the major foundations and non-profit organizations in Baltimore:

Baltimore Community Foundation:

The Baltimore Community Foundation is a philanthropic foundation created by and for the people of Greater Baltimore, where many donors join together to make the region they love a better place, today and for future generations.

Our goals:

- **Build a civic endowment,** a permanent source of philanthropic funding for the greater Baltimore region,

- **Help donors** plan and carry out their charitable giving in Baltimore, the region, and across the country,

- **Work in partnership** with other foundations, public agencies and the business sector, bringing a consistent voice of leadership to critical civic issues.

Our vision:

Baltimore boasts a growing economy, where all have an opportunity to thrive. Our action agenda organizes grants, initiatives and advocacy around this vision.

Our mission:

Inspire donors to achieve their charitable goals from generation to generation and to improve the quality of life in the Baltimore region through grant making, enlightened civic leadership and strategic investments.

Our values:

- BCF is **trustworthy**. We strive to earn, build and maintain trust among donors, grantees, staff, trustees and the greater Baltimore community.

- BCF is **inclusive**. We incorporate diversity, equity and inclusion into all aspects of our work.

- BCF is **entrepreneurial**. We articulate and implement a bold, inspiring vision for Baltimore by leveraging resources in creative ways.

The Open Society Institute: Mission & Values December 2011

Our Mission
- The Open Society Foundations work to build vibrant and tolerant societies whose governments are accountable and open to the participation of all people.
- We seek to strengthen the rule of law; respect for human rights, minorities, and a diversity of opinions; democratically elected governments; and a civil society that helps keep government power in check.

- We help to shape public policies that assure greater fairness in political, legal, and economic systems and safeguard fundamental rights.
- We implement initiatives to advance justice, education, public health, and independent media.
- We build alliances across borders and continents on issues such as corruption and freedom of information.
- Working in every part of the world, the Open Society Foundations place a high priority on protecting and improving the lives of people in marginalized communities.

Our Values

- We believe in fundamental human rights, dignity, and the rule of law.
- We believe in a society where all people are free to participate fully in civic, economic, and cultural life.
- We believe in addressing inequalities that cut across multiple lines, including race, class, gender, sexual orientation, and citizenship.
- We believe in holding those in power accountable for their actions and in increasing the power of historically excluded groups.
- We believe in helping people and communities press for change on their own behalf.
- We believe in responding quickly and flexibly to the most critical threats to open society.

- We believe in taking on controversial issues and supporting bold, innovative solutions that address root causes and advance systemic change.
- We believe in encouraging critical debate and respecting diverse opinions.

The Abell Foundation:

The Abell Foundation, formerly known as The A.S. Abell Company Foundation, was established on December 31, 1953. The Foundation was established by the late Harry C. Black, philanthropist and then chairman of the board of the A.S. Abell Company, the former publisher of *The Baltimore Sun*.

Initially the Foundation provided gifts primarily to hospitals, educational institutions, arts organizations, and human services organizations. At the time of the name change to The Abell Foundation in 1986, the Foundation's agenda became far more broad and ambitious. Under the 27-year leadership of Robert C. Embry, Jr. as president, The Abell Foundation has become the largest private foundation serving only Maryland. Its mission continues to be to act as an agent of change, with special emphasis on education, workforce development, health and human services, community development, criminal justice and addictions, conservation and environment, and arts and culture. The Foundation's work has expanded from being focused solely on grant making to include research and publications on important policy issues, and direct investments in early stage companies that offer significant social and economic benefits.

Since its establishment 28 years ago, The Abell Foundation has contributed more than $263,000,000 to the community. Its assets have increased from $113 million to more than $350 million.

The Baltimore Family League:

The Family League of Baltimore leads, develops and implements collaborative solutions to help struggling, hard-working Baltimore families and children achieve their dreams of a better life. The Family League was established in 1991 as the Baltimore's Local Management Board to manage and deploy government funds that strengthen children and families. The organization serves as an architect of change, leveraging relationships with public and private entities, as well as convening stakeholders from local government, the funding community and direct service organizations to bring together financial support and a shared vision for education and nutrition that benefit the children and families of Baltimore.

Safe and Sound Campaign:

- The Safe and Sound Campaign is Baltimore's movement to improve conditions for children, youth and families.

- People have come together from all over the city to make this a reality. They are standing up to say that conditions are unacceptable for too many of Baltimore's kids. And they are taking action to turn things around — so all children have the opportunity to be their best and have realistic expectations for a bright future.
- Baltimore's Safe and Sound Campaign is made up of everyday people — thousands from all walks of life — who want to make sure our kids succeed. It is a Campaign with a clear vision and meaningful goals. And through its citywide strategies, it is working.

Throughout the mission and vision statements of these institutions you see the same general theme of wanting to help people who are disadvantaged. Even in the Open Society Baltimore statement there is a sentence which mentions that they believe in helping people press for change on their own behalf. I think it's worth noting that OSI is probably the most radical of the foundations in Baltimore, but all of the other elements of their mission exemplify the concept of liberal multiculturalism that often crowds out the call for independent Black institutions. Without the objective of developing independent Black institutions being embedded in the work of these foundations and non-profits, the default position is to depend on a white dominated civil society to protect the interest of Black people. This has obviously not been an effective paradigm for Black empowerment.

Liberal multiculturalism is a term which refers to the way that issues of Black Liberation are crowded out by liberal activists and intellectuals making broad calls for justice. Typically the language used to articulate this broad vision of justice is structured on the notion of inclusion. The generally idea is that the goal of those seeking justice is greater social inclusion in the American body politic. This concept of inclusion has the effect of crowding out the call for an autonomous economic, social and political apparatus for Black people. For example, people often articulate the call for Civil Rights during the 1960's as a call for social inclusion. The 1964 Civil Right Act exemplified the idea that the primary remedy to issues of racial inequality is to take down all the barriers that keep Black people from being included in the American mainstream. What is interesting is that this notion of social inclusion is often used to disavow the need for independent Black institutions. People have said things to me like, "I thought the point of Civil Rights was for everyone to come together?" This sentiment if often deployed to make those of us advocating for independent Black institutions seem divisive and hateful. Social inclusion is also used to undermine Black people's ability to talk specifically about our own issues. It puts us in a bind wherein conversations meant to address Black people, constantly get railroaded by people who would rather talk broadly about social justice than attempt to focus on the specific demands of Black people. People often say things like "Black people are not the only people who are oppressed." These two sentiments are buttressed by the idea that social inclusion is the solution to fixing the problems Black people face. What has happened historically is that the organizing methods, the crafting of campaigns and the logic of the Civil Rights Movement has been used to advance justice for other people more than it has for Black people. The Women's Liberation Movement, the Gay Rights Movement, the Anti-War Movement, the Disabilities Rights Movement and many others greatly benefited from the gains of the Civil Rights Movement. What is interesting is that women get Women's Rights, LGBT people get Gay Rights, but Civil Rights are supposed to be for everyone. When Black people speak specifically about our issues we are told that we should not just advocate for Black Liberation but for every one's liberation. This is a burden that other groups are not subject to. No one tells (white) women that they aren't the only ones that are oppressed when they speak about gender oppression, no one tells Latinos that they are not the only ones suffering under racist immigration laws when they advocate for things like the Dream Act, so why are we held to this burden? This is what we call liberal multiculturalism, which uses the broad call for justice to crowd out the specific demands of Black people. It is a liberal form of anti-blackness that is propagated by all of the missions of the organizations mentioned above.

I want to dig a little deeper into this Civil Rights concept to help expose the ways that liberal multiculturalism is foundational to way that non-profits participate in this liberal form of anti-blackness. Martin Luther King Jr. is often used as the compass that white people evoke to navigate their thinking about racism in America. In fact, the famous "I Have a Dream Speech" is often used to advance the ethos of liberal multiculturalism. People quote the line about being judged not "by the color of their skin but by the content of their character." This is used over and over again to erase radicalism from King's legacy. Two elements of this quotation are deceptive. First, this line is referencing a fantasy - King is articulating a world where people are able to live without being discriminated against. Dr. King was not offering this as a solution to the problem of racism, but as a fantasy that he aspired to. Does the dream of living in a world without discrimination mean that people should not celebrate and be proud of their cultural heritage? Of course not. Many of the speeches King gave toward the end of his life reflected on the importance of being proud of being Black. He wrote about the importance of Black people developing power to challenge the oppression that we faced. Dr. King, in his book *Where Do We Go From Here,* says:

> *"Black Power, in its broad and positive meaning, is a call to black people to amass the political and economic strength to achieve their legitimate goals. No one can deny that the Negro is in dire need of*

131

this kind of legitimate power. Indeed, one of the great problems that the Negro confronts is his lack of power. From the old plantations of the South to the newer ghettos of the North, the Negro has been confined to a life of voicelessness and powerlessness. ...The plantation and the ghetto were created by those who had power both to confine those who had no power and to perpetuate their powerlessness. The problem of transforming the ghetto is, therefore, a problem of power – a confrontation between the forces of power demanding change and the forces of power dedicated to preserving the status quo."

The broad notion of Civil Rights which is typically evoked by white liberals is an immature iteration of justice that does not recognize the realities of white power. Dr. King remarked on this in his speech "Black Power defined":

"The nettlesome task of Negroes today is to discover how to organize our strength into compelling power so that government cannot elude our demands. We must develop, from strength, a situation in which the government finds it wise and prudent to collaborate with us. It would be the height of naiveté to wait passively until the administration had somehow been infused with such blessings of good will that it implored us for our programs.

We must frankly acknowledge that in past years our creativity and imagination were not employed in learning how to develop power. We found a method in nonviolent protest that worked, and we employed it enthusiastically. We did not have leisure to probe for a deeper understanding of its laws and lines of development. Although our actions were bold and crowned with successes, they were substantially improvised and spontaneous. They attained the goals set for them but carried the blemishes of our inexperience."

The point here is that the use of one line out of one speech is often used to mute out the larger point of Black self-determination. This phenomenon is a tool of liberal multiculturalism. Reducing King's message to a broad vision of people of all races holding hands crowds out his message of developing independent Black institutions.

The second element that is deceptive about the use of the "I Have a Dream" speech is that most people don't understand that moment in its historical context. Dr. John Henrik Clarke once said that the March on Washington and the "I Have a Dream" speech was the beginning of the decline of the Civil Right Movement. John F. Kennedy was terrified by the idea of thousands of Black people coming together to protest in Washington DC. When he realized that he could not stop it he sought to co-opt it. There was a meeting before the March on Washington at the Carlyle Hotel in New York City which was owned by the Kennedy family.　　At the request of President Kennedy, Steven Kerry who was a leader in the philanthropic world pulled together what was called the "Big Six." This group was made up of the heads of the major Civil Rights organizations. They formed the Leadership Conference on Civil Rights which acted as a vehicle for providing philanthropic money to these organizations. This allowed white philanthropy to have control over the activities of these organizations in such a way that it could contain the actions of the movement. The Commission was given $800,000 to split up between the Civil Rights organizations and were promised $700,000 more after the March on Washington. This co-option of the Civil Rights Movement by white liberals was pointed out by Malcolm X at the time and is the model that continues to be used to co-opt Black Liberation. It is likely that this is one of the immaturities that King spoke about in *Where Do We Go From Here* which undermined the cultivation of authentic power. The use of the white liberal ethos of the "I Have a Dream" speech is the substance of liberal multiculturalism in America that renders invisible the way that white people use philanthropy to contain and control authentic, grassroots Black Leadership.

Another structural impediment inherent in the non-profit structure is the need for technical assessments and data. The kind of overly technical data which is often asked of non-profit organizations in order to receive funding requires money that most Black grassroots organizations don't have.   This gives an inherent bias toward white people who typically have greater access to resources than Black people.   Auditors and firms that do professional assessments are expensive and benefit from providing their specialized services in the status quo.   The idea that organizations should have ways of measuring their effectiveness is important, but the high priority placed on assessment has the effect of making it difficult for Black people, who often have less access to resources, to gain access to grant funding.   Those who are truly interested in empowering Black people should take this in consideration in how grants are structured and dispensed.   This may also require changes in federal regulations for how government agencies structure and dispense grants so that grassroots organizations have more access to them.   Some might argue that changing these regulation risk corruption.   But the status quo is fettered with legalized corruption.   Non-profits are making money off of Black misery, without having to produce the kinds of results needed to transform our communities.   I would rather have to worry about rooting out corruption in a context where people who are of and from the communities being served have more access to resources, than the legalized corruption that allows people to profit off of our suffering.

Another related but a separate issue is the way that people with professional degrees are seen as being experts on the issues that Black people face.   Much of the training that people receive in major educational institutions is structured in a way that is embedded in the same notion of Black inferiority mentioned above. These professionals may become masters at navigating the academy, but are not taught the skills necessary to effectively transform the institutions that oppress Black people. Many people in the communities most directly affected by white supremacy are capable of managing and operating organizations that seek to improve the quality of life of Black people. What often happens is that they don't have the advanced degrees that people in non-profit organizations have (and therefore expect when they make hiring decisions of their own). As a result, Black people in non-profits are often relegated to being the subordinates of credentialed white directors and managers. As subordinates, they are not able to make policy decisions even though they may be eminently qualified on the basis of their experience and track record of work in the community. This also happens to Black people who do have advanced degrees. Those of us with college education are often represented as being inferior to our white counterparts until we prove otherwise, even then we are not given the same level of confidence in our abilities that our white counterparts receive. I want to be clear, not all information gained from formal education is useless, but we should not view white people as better at leading and directing organizations aimed at addressing our issues.

Another way that the notion of Black inferiority manifests itself in the non-profit industrial complex is the inability for people in charge of these organizations to see strength in the communities they attempt to serve. Here in Baltimore, you rarely hear from those operating and supporting non-profit work that they aim to build on the strengths that already exist in the community. Organizations like the Family League of Baltimore, which is tasked with providing resources and programs that are designed to help families and children rarely refer to the strength of the community which they are attempting to build on. They typically base their programs on the idea that there need to be interventions in the community's affairs, instead of supporting the work that is already happening. The dominant narrative that is cast over Black communities is that there is nothing of value that goes on without white oversight. We are represented as pathological and in need of intervention to help address our pathological behavior. If you look on the Family League's website or their materials, you will not find any acknowledgement that they are taking the lead from people in the community who are currently trying to improve their own quality of life. This is reflected in their mission statement above. This lack of acknowledgement belies the arrogance that is endemic in non-profit work, particularly by white people who have internalized notions of Black inferiority. The idea that you can prescribe solutions to a people whose culture and history you have not immersed yourself in is an attitude that is taken toward Black people because of the deep-seeded notion of Black inferiority that animates so much of the non-profit work here in Baltimore. The Family League of Baltimore is not exceptional in this regard; it is just a clear example of how the non-profit industrial complex functions.

Another instance of the non-profit industrial complex here in Baltimore is the Public Safety Compact. The technical aspects of compacts are quite complicated, but the general idea behind this program is that when people are released from prison they are referred to the Public Safety Compact where they are provided with programs and services designed to keep them from re-offending. If the person who is referred doesn't re-offend within a certain amount of time, the Public Safety Compact gets a certain percentage of the money that the state saved from not having to house that person in detention. On its face this sounds like a great idea. However, two problems exist and both are rooted in the non-profit industrial complex. First, these resources require that someone gets incarcerated to begin with. Whereas investment in community preventive services might stop some folks from being jailed in the first place, the compact is invested in incarceration itself. In many cases, waiting until a person is incarcerated to provide services is too late; they may have already passed up on important opportunities that would keep them out of the penal system. The second problem with this model is that the Public Safety Compact here in Baltimore is managed by the Safe and Sound Campaign, whose executive director is Hathaway Ferebee. She is a white woman who we criticized a couple of years ago regarding the issue of non-profits co-opting the fight against the Youth Jail. Her ability to direct large amount of resources to programs that she sees thinks are effective is a tremendous amount of power. A person who is not of and from the communities being served should not be able to make such an important decision about the livelihood of the community. This is not a personal critique, but a statement of the way in which white people are often given the authority to make major decisions that affect Black people in communities that are being served.

White people often think that they are giving us a gift by having empathy for us. They think that doing work in Black communities entitles them to leadership positions in our institutions. Let me say this very clearly, we don't NEED white people. This isn't to say that there are not ways in which white people can be allies to Black Liberation, or that we shouldn't welcome beneficial partnerships. But it is important that everyone regardless of your race understands that we don't NEED white people. If white people disappeared we would be fine. There are many people that will have trouble with this statement because it seems mean and hateful. This is often how notions of Black independence are represented, as being hateful toward whites. This is certainly not the case here. It is important that I say that we don't need white people because it is from this point that we can develop a healthy notion of what it will take to actually eradicate racism. Black people have to be able to imagine a world where white people are not necessary for us to be able to live a good quality of life. Just as white people think that they are necessary parts of our liberation, Black people have internalized this notion that we need white people. This conceptual hang-up often keeps us from focusing on developing our own institutions to defend our own interest.

Some people at this point may feel that this kind of critique of white people who profess to be committed to empowering Black people may be tremendously harsh and unprecedented, but this critique is as old as the concept of racism itself. Martin Delany in *The Condition, Elevation, Emigration, and Destiny of the Colored People of the United States* (1852) remarks about the position of Black people in the Anti-Slavery movement:

> "It is true, that the 'Liberator' office, in Boston, has got Elijah
> Smith, a colored youth, at the cases--the "Standard," in New York, a
> young colored man, and the "Freeman," in Philadelphia, William Still,
> another, in the publication office, as "packing clerk"; yet these are
> but three out of the hosts that fill these offices in their various
> departments, all occupying places that could have been, and as we once
> thought, would have been, easily enough, occupied by colored men.

Indeed, we can have no other idea about anti-slavery in this country,

than that the legitimate persons to fill any and every position about an

anti-slavery establishment are colored persons. Nor will it do to argue

in extenuation, that white men are as justly entitled to them as colored

men; because white men do not from _necessity_ become anti-slavery men

in order to get situations; they being white men, may occupy any

position they are capable of filling--in a word, their chances are

endless, every avenue in the country being opened to them. They do not

therefore become abolitionists, for the sake of employment--at least, it

is not the song that anti-slavery sung, in the first love of the new

faith, proclaimed by its disciples.

And if it be urged that colored men are incapable as yet to fill these

positions, all that we have to say is, that the cause has fallen far

short; almost equivalent to a failure, of a tithe, of what it promised to do in half the period of its existence, to this time, if it have not

as yet, now a period of twenty years, raised up colored men enough, to

fill the offices within its patronage. We think it is not unkind to say,

if it had been half as faithful to itself, as it should have been--its

professed principles we mean; it could have reared and tutored from

childhood, colored men enough by this time, for its own especial

purpose."

The idea that a Black person would criticize white people who form the Anti-Slavery movement during the 1850s may seem unfathomable, but the legacy of white folks taking the lead on issues facing Black folks, and not thinking that Black people have the capacity to lead major institutional efforts is a trend that runs throughout the history of people in the US. Even here in Baltimore this is the logic that governs the non-profit industry here.

One very good example of this is in our interaction with the Baltimore Algebra Project (BAP). The Algebra Project is a national organization founded by Bob Moses that has chapters all over the United States. Baltimore's chapter is one of the largest and most active. In 2008, many students we had mentored in debate were also a part of BAP. At the time BAP was led by two white male advisers. A few of the students we came in contact with identified themselves as communists. These were Black students who were interested in joining debate and being activist. This communist designation alarmed me because it seems tremendously out of place. The idea of communism as a political identity was not something indigenous to the culture and environment that Black youth find themselves in here in Baltimore. I knew that this had to come from somewhere. What I later found out was that the gentlemen who were the white advisers were heavily influencing the ideological perspectives of young people in the organization. Luckily the students that I had mentored in debate, who had previously joined BAP were close to the youth who were proclaiming to be communists and helped to facilitate amazing conversations that eventually changed the students' perspectives. We were attempting to impart the idea that developing independent Black institutions as the primary political objective should replace their allegiance to communism. We explained to them that communists have a history of using Black people's issues to support the political power and intellectual project of white people who profess to be our friends. For example, during the Cold War the Soviet Union solicited support from people like WEB DuBois and Paul Robeson to support their position in their clash with America. Even though they would speak about the abuses of Black people by white Americans they were not willing to lend resources to Black people for the purposes of building autonomous

Black intuitions although they gave resources to Black people for supporting Communist efforts and organizations. Even most abolitionists were not truly interested in equality with Black people. According to Carter G. Woodson in his book "The Century of Negro Migration" he says that many of the white people who advocated for slavery to be abolished did not want to live with or near Black people. The usual response to this by the students was that this framework would exclude the white advisers whom they had grown to develop affective relationships with. They remarked on the food that they had gotten from these advisers, they referred to the rides that they had been given, and the numerous favors that the advisers had done for them as arguments against Pan-Afrikan Nationalism (the idea of Black political, social, and economic independence). What is important to note is that their advisers' kindnesses, even if motivated by genuine good intentions, are not responsive to the need for independent Black Institutions. Yet it seemed appropriate to the students to mention it because they had developed such a close emotional connections to their advisers. They had trouble separating the importance of having institutional control over our communities from their interpersonal relationships with white people. They eventually began to understand that white people who were unwilling to acknowledge the importance of Black leadership on issues facing Black people where merely using us to their own political ends. This also played itself out in the relationship that we began to develop with one of the white advisers in

BAP. Over time we were able to dialogue in a way that was eventually able let him appreciate the importance of Black Leadership. What is interesting is that many of my elders know this particular adviser and dislike him for his use of Black children to prop up a white liberal approach to addressing social justice. What I found was that the dialogue that we have been engaged in for almost 6 years now has been helpful in creating a context for the students of BAP have greater connection to Black adults who understand the importance of the development of independent Black institutions. This demonstrates what can happen when white people make themselves willing to defer to Black leadership. This is the only appropriate position for white people to have in the struggle for Black Liberation. White people who are willing step out of the way of Black Leadership and support it are the only white people fit to claim to be interested in improving the life of Black people in America.

Spectacular Blackness
By Dayvon Love

The notion of the white gaze can seem to be an elusive and esoteric concept. The purpose of this article is to develop a working notion of the white gaze and its practical application in the realm of social and political activism on the issues facing Black people in the US. All of the representations that are highly circulated through our society are transmitted through a cultural lens rooted in white supremacy and European domination. This may seem to be a harsh characterization of the images and representations present in mass media and popular culture but, after we have examined the insidious ways that white supremacy manifests itself, it will become clear that this is the most analytically precise way to characterize the collective American imagination.

Let's define some terms and the relationship that these terms have to each other. This will help to conceptually place the analysis that will take place later on. White supremacy is the central organizing principle on which civil society is structured. It is a political system that organizes society in such a way that the collective social, political, economic interest of white people are reinforced and protected at the expense of people of color. Culture is a totality of thought and practice from which a people sustains itself, celebrates itself and introduces itself to history and humanity. This means that culture is not merely song and dance, but is the lens from which the world is interpreted. It is the lens that allows a people to navigate the world in a way that is accountable to their material relationship to the world and the collective personality of a people. The relationship between these two ideas is that white supremacy is a structure that places at the center the European cultural ethos. The lens from which Americans are socialized to interpret the world is one that is essentially European in its epistemological orientation. Ultimately what this means is that we are socialized to see the world in such a way that the centrality of European cultural ideas (enlightenment), and social, economic, and political superiority of white people seem rational. For example, it seems rational that we refer to WWI and WWII as world wars. This designation doesn't strike most people as odd. But if you think about what a world war means, it would imply that most of the world is at war. In both of the wars referred to as world wars, there were European countries (with the exception of Japan in the latter part of WWII) that were at war. The wars referred to as world wars are really events where Europeans declared war with each other. This excludes Africa, Asia and South America in a way that suggests history happens primarily in Europe. It is arrogant to call these wars 'world wars' yet to the average American the notion of WWI and WWII make perfect sense and demonstrates the way in which the centrality of European cultural ideas and the social, political and economic superiority of white people are made to seem rational. This is just one of many examples of how the lens from which people are taught to interpret the world prop up notions of white supremacy.

The notion of the white gaze describes how images and representations of Black people are interpolated by white people in a way that reinforces their power and status as normal in civil society. For instance, minstrel shows in the early 20th century demonstrate how white people produced representations of Black people as buffoons, lazy, unintelligent, shiftless, etc. that reinforce notions of their own superiority. This continues today as we look at the hip hop industry which has been increasingly commodified in a way that is marketable to the suburban white kids who are the primary consumers of commercial hip hop. Tricia Rose's work on hip hop is the most accurate analysis on the issue of the implications of the commercialization of hip hop. But I don't want to spend a lot of time fleshing out that argument and if you want to learn more about the commodification of hip hop I suggest you read her work *Hip Hop Wars*. What I want to focus on here is the fact that the white gaze is the ever-present active process of white interpolation on Black bodies in such a way that we are "re-presented" to ourselves in ways that reinscribe white supremacy. These representations permeate all aspects of society, even spaces that seem radical.

The concept that I want to forward in the context of our discussion of the white gaze is the notion of the "spectacularization of blackness." Black people are rendered the most visible and valuable in our society when we are spectacles. It is very important that I clarify here that when I say the term spectacular in this context, I'm not talking about spectacular in the sense of something being amazing, or terrific, but spectacular in the sense of being a spectacle, something that brings affective meaning, or enjoyment. This is evident in the way that Black people are often seen as athletes and entertainers in popular culture, but not often represented in other context where we are not spectacles. The notion of the spectacularization of blackness has had a tremendously devastating impact on the way in which Black people have mobilized for political empowerment.

Saidiya Hartman's book *Scenes of Subjection* speaks brilliantly to the nature of the spectacularization of Black suffering and its implication in the way that this reinforces white supremacy.

> "While Rankin attempts to ameliorate the insufficiency of feeling before the spectacle of the other's suffering, this insufficiency is, in fact, displaced rather than remedied by his standing in. Likewise, this attempt exacerbates the distance between the readers and those suffering by literally removing the slave from view as pain is brought close. Moreover, we need to consider whether the identification forged at the site of suffering confirms black humanity at the peril of reinforcing racist assumptions of limited sentience, in that the humanity of the enslaved and the violence of the

institution can only be brought into view by extreme examples of incineration and dismemberment or by placing white bodies at risk. What does it mean that the violence of slavery or the pained experience of the enslaved, if discernible, is only so in the most heinous and grotesque examples and not the quotidian routines of slavery? As well, is not the difficulty of empathy related to both the devaluation and the valuation of black life?" Pg. 20-21

Many of the narratives that are used to represent the horrors of slavery revolve around the spectacular horrors of beatings and whippings etc. This narrative and representational emphasis on the spectacular violence of enslavement, has the effect of obscuring the way that the everyday framework of suffering that is the structural position of the slave is a form of brutality in itself. There are day to day routines that constitute the violence of enslavement that are misunderstood as a footnote to the way we understand the oppression of enslaved people. When we focus on the spectacle of suffering, this has three major implications on how we organize ourselves.

The first implication is that our bodies are marked as sites of empathy. Empathy is the way in which white people can identify with the suffering Black people face. We become objects of the white imagination. We become the wretched oppressed minority that needs white redemption in order to be liberated from our misery. What happens is that white people don't actually identify with the suffering - instead they identify with what their own imaginations register as the suffering that they can know and observe. Empathy has the effect of making white people think that they can transcend the corporeal limitations of their bodies and locate themselves as being a part of Black suffering. One key element of the white imagination is that white people are convinced of their own indispensability to Black people's struggle for freedom and therefore project all of their ideas and feelings onto Black bodies and Black issues.

A concrete example of the way this effects organizing is through much of the language and framework from which the struggle for social justice is framed. Much of the left has established a canon of literature and ideas that are used in radical circles to qualify someone as sufficiently radical. If you are radical you must read Foucault, Derrida, Marx, De Beauvoir, Sartre, Agamben, and others. What all of these theorist have in common is that they place the notion of resisting power as central to the project of challenging oppression. You will hear many people of color taught that the objective of our work is to fight racism and global oppression. This emphasis crowds out and at times discourages the notion of building up independent institutions to develop the power necessary to protect ourselves from the oppression lodged at us by civil society. Many of us get so consumed in this discourse that we become obsessed with the idea of fighting racism abstractly, but spend very little time building the institutions needed to effectively empower ourselves and fight white supremacy. This all comes as a result of the way that white interpolation "re-presents" our bodies and our issues in ways that we internalize as our own. We need to reject white people's framing of our issues and embrace our own indigenous thoughts about how we should move politically. White people frame us as needing their empathy and redress in order to achieve justice and then we often reproduce this discourse in our efforts at organizing. This discourse reinforces a narcissism in which we talk primarily about how to change the minds and hearts of white people, instead of focusing on how we can build independent institutions that we can use as a basis for protecting our interest. This doesn't mean that we should not criticize and demand things from white society, but this should not be the prevailing framework for how we do our work. We need to focus on organizing our own power instead of focusing on the white left mantra of resisting power.

The second major implication of the spectacularization of Blackness has to do with the kinds of efforts that Black people organize around. When the George Zimmerman and Trayvon Martin incident hit mainstream media it created an uproar. People of all races had very extreme opinions about what this incident represented about the state of racism in America. What was interesting was the ways in which many organizations and individuals rallied around this issue. What made this interesting to me was that this was not a new issue in our community. Our people have been killed by police in America for decades. This is an ongoing problem that we face every day. So the question is what made this particular case worthy of the kind of attention that it was receiving in the mainstream media? I don't think there is one single answer to this question. Some credit the major rallies that took place to get the case to be tried, others credit the way that social media has revolutionized activism. What I want to focus on is the way that this case captivated the hearts and minds of people all over the country. The incident between Trayvon Martin and George Zimmerman served as a national spectacle. The competing narratives, and the drama that was often associated with the incident and the trial, took center stage in the minds of Americans. The support and attention given to the family of Trayvon Martin was extraordinary in many ways and demonstrated the power that Black unity can produced if we are deliberate in our attempts to combat white supremacy.

Before I go on I want to be very clear. The lives of Black people who are killed at the hands of law enforcement and/or vigilantes are important and deserve our political and social attention. But the spectacularized representations of Black men who are assailed by civil society have the effect of rendering invisible the suffering the Black people face that is less spectacular, but just as devastating. One very important example of this is the persistent nature of sexual assault and sex trafficking in our community. Girls and woman all over this country of all races and ethnicities are victimized by sexual assault and sex trafficking. But Black girls have been over represented among minors who are trafficked and abused. This should be tremendously alarming to those of us committed to the liberation of people of African Descent. Yet we often respond more intensely to spectacular narratives and representation of suffering than to the constant suffering that is less spectacular. People all over the country organized around the tragedy of Trayvon Martin's murder, but there is not nearly the same fever around building the kind of institutions that would help to eradicate sexual assault and human trafficking from our communities. Sexual assault and domestic violence are not anomalies that are isolated incidents; this is a systemic problem that exists in our communities that undermines the ability to produce healthy people and healthy communities. The devaluation of Black women's bodies is a broad and pervasive phenomenon that goes back to the way in which Black women's bodies were captive to the fetishization of their bodies by white men during slavery. bell hooks in her essay "Selling Hot Pussy" explains that these representations of Black women's bodies have been seared into the collective consciousness of Americans. These representations depict Black woman's bodies as sexual objects, as over-sexed and having insatiable sexual appetites. This myth is used to justify the exploitation of Black women's bodies and displace the responsibility of those who engage in acts of sexual aggression toward Black women onto the contrived notions of Black women's overzealous sexual desires.

If we juxtapose the way in which the lynching of Black men was made a public spectacle, versus the highly private ways in which Black women suffered sexual violence at the hands of white men, we can see how those same manifestations today in the kinds of violence that capture our attention and the kinds of violence that gets swept under the rug. Lynchings were public events, entertainments where people took pictures and brought their children to witness the lynching. David Marriot in his book *On Black Men* explains very well how the image of lynching has had dramatic psycho-social implications for how Black suffering is represented in civil society. In many ways, the narrative of Black men being shot and killed by police and/or vigilantes occupies the same space on our imagination that lynching occupied during Jim Crow. Just as the sexual violence that Black women experience does not register as spectacular it is relegated to 'background noise,' something we never organize around as a community. This kind of suffering is rendered invisible because it is not accompanied by the spectacular representations that the white gaze interpolates onto our bodies and our issues. Not only does this spectacularization have the effect of rendering other forms of violence against Black people invisible, but it also obscures the fundamentally systemic nature of the problem of police brutality. We should not see the Trayvon Martin incident as an isolated extreme event of racial violence, but as a manifestation of the very structure of civil society.

The last major implication of the spectacularization of Blackness is that it foregrounds the identity of Blackness in our narratives of suffering and oppression. What this means is that the notion of authentic Blackness is framed as being those who are closest in proximity to suffering. The narratives of suffering are what white liberal use to justify the use of Black bodies for their political and intellectual projects. If we are characterized primarily by our suffering then we are able to be incorporated into other people's political programs. You see this in many left-leaning circles that often represent Black life as defined by suffering. In fact, if asked to think about the word poverty, many people would have images of Black people in their minds. Many of the programs of the left, including things like welfare, reproductive health services, social services, and many non-profit organizations use and deploy this imagery in order to create a market for their programs. The use of Black faces on promotional materials for such institutions take advantage of the way that Blackness is assumed to mean Black suffering. We can also see this in the way that Black death is tremendously marketable. Popular culture is rife with images of Black death and Black suffering. When we look at the news we are likely to see stories of Black death and violence. This gets so ingrained in how we understand what it means to be Black that we cannot see Blackness as something that has positive characteristics. The more downtrodden one is the more Black they are considered to be. This creates a standard for Blackness that frames out images of strength in Blackness.

Blackness is stigmatized as primarily pathological. This creates the conceptual block that keeps people from being able to see strength and intelligence in Black people. This leads many of us to think that we need white people involved in our political struggles in order for us to have strong political infrastructure.

What some may say is that if white men where the primary people assaulting Black women that there would be more of an outcry from the Black community. I want to address this so that this idea does not get in the way of the larger point I am trying to make. First of all, it shouldn't matter who is assaulting Black women, if Black girls and Black women are being assaulted it should be a priority, but because it isn't accompanied by spectacular representations we don't give it the attention that it deserves. Secondly, white society is extremely troubled by Black violence. You hear the term Black on Black crime as a phrase that stands in for the way in which violence perpetuated by Black men against each other is made a spectacle in our popular culture. Some of our own people will organize around stop the violence rallies, but how often do we have public demonstrations against sexual assault and sex trafficking? This again is the effect of the spectacularization of Blackness dictating the way in which we organize politically. My point here is that Black male violence against one another is spectacularized and given attention, but the sexual violence that Black women face is not given attention and therefore not enough political organizing by Black people is done around this issue.

Some may say that the solution to this problem is to raise the issue of sexual assault to a national spectacle, but this doesn't get at the root issue of how the white gaze operates on our bodies and our issues and ultimately dictates how we move politically. We must learn to develop a framework for political organizing that is rooted in our own authentic, indigenous experience in doing work in the communities in which we reside. The media, the academy and non-profit organizations should not be the guiding forces behind how we represent the issues in the community. We should be organizing on the ground with grassroots organizations to address the issues right in front of us. One of my mentors, Wmalimu Locy Lummuba once explained to me a metaphor that best describes the orientation of the political organizing that needs to take place. He says that if there are rats attempting to get in a baby's crib, there are people who will focus on trying to find the rat hole and close it up. He said the priority should be getting the rat out of the baby's crib before we start trying to close up the rat hole. We must focus on building our communities first before we devote too much attention to the national mainstream that distracts us from actually fighting forces of oppression in our communities.

Section Two

Fighting the Youth Jail
By Dayvon Love

Background

Juveniles in Maryland's adult prisons have been subject to horrendous conditions for many years now. Due to a federal decree, the State of Maryland was required to develop a plan to address these conditions. As a result, the state under the leadership of Governor Martin O'Malley decided that it was necessary to build an entirely new juvenile detention facility. Debate over this Youth Jail, slated to cost $104 million, was largely kept silent in mainstream political conversations.

Before the fight against the Youth Jail materialized the idea of building a new jail did not seem politically controversial. The first real agitation on the issue of the Youth Jail came from Pastor Heber M. Brown III of Pleasant Hope Baptist Church, the author of a blog called "Faith and Action" (that has since been attacked by "bots" and shut down). In this blog he posted an article about the *Prison Industrial Complex* and the new proposed jail as an extension of this assault on Black people. He then posted a picture of the Baltimore legislators who voted to move forward with the construction of the new jail. One of these legislators called him immediately to discuss the issue. According to Rev. Brown, the conversation consisted mostly of the delegate expressing that he didn't realize the severe implications of a new jail. From this understanding that many proponents

160

didn't fully understand the issue, Rev. Brown, Jamye Wooten of Kinetics, LBS, the Baltimore Algebra Project (BAP), and many other Black grassroots organizations decided to organize an event called "Youth Justice Sunday." This marked our intension to fight the Jail from the grassroots. Simultaneously, white-led foundations and non-profits were organizing to converge onto the issue. Through a series of back and forth meetings, conflicts, community organizing, lobbying legislators, radio appearances, social media campaigns, and more, we were able to force the state to abandon its plan to build the Youth Jail in January of 2013. To narrate everything that happened during this effort would require its own book. I want to spend the time in this piece reflecting on significant moments during the fight against the youth jail and the application of the political theories advanced in the previous section.

Where are the Black adults?

At the beginning of this fight I was 23. I was fortunate enough to have mentors who are Black people experienced with social justice issues facing Black people. The abundance of Black elders as mentors helped to craft my thinking about the kind of organizing that needed to happen to empower Black people. The central element to effective organization for Black liberation is the struggle for Black self-determination. We need to build capacity and build institutions that allow us to address our own issues on our own terms. This was my framework in entering the fight against the youth jail.

One dynamic that I became increasingly troubled by as I moved through Baltimore's self-proclaimed social justice communities was the overwhelming presence of white adults and Black youth. Most of the adult advisors were white adults from foundations or non-profits, and most of the youth were Black students from Baltimore. There were a few meetings where I mentioned this dynamic openly. The response that I often got from the white adults was that they had tried to reach out to Black organizations for support, but no one reached back.

I want to pause here and talk for a bit about the limitations that typically young white non-profit folks have. In order to organize effectively you need to have established networks and connections to people in the community. If you are a transplant into a community it takes time for people to trust you and to get to know who you are. This also limits your ability to know who you don't know. Many of the white people (typically young white women) working for these non-profit organizations fighting against the jail had no idea about the extent to which they didn't know who the players are in the community. This made the white adults who were involved in the fight against the jail ill-equipped to carry out a truly community-led effort.

There is a long history of white liberals coming into the Black community and trying to take leadership of initiatives that primarily affect Black people. This continues to be the case. In fact, the non-profits that joined the fight against the Youth Jail were doing exactly that. This probably explains why Black adults (particularly elders) were not very responsive to the call from these non-profit organizations to join forces. This created a situation where the non-profit organizations could only attract Black *youth* to their cause because young people tend not to have this historical context and perspective. What was happening was that the Black youth were literally being used to give legitimacy to the white liberal fight against the youth jail.

Because of the inter-generational issues that we have as Black people (which requires another piece to adequately address), Black youth tend to be estranged from Black adults. This estrangement leaves the door open for white liberals to come in and develop the kind of affective relationships with Black students that enable them to recruit these Black youth to their organizations. The cultivation of these relationships usually includes buying pizza, paying for expensive trips, allowing youth to have profanity-laced conversations with them, and giving them affirmation about how intelligent they, among many other things. Because we live in a society that is rooted in Black inferiority, white affirmation and attention are very powerful in getting students to become attached to white liberal causes and organizations. I have seen students develop a sense of pride that is purely based off of the affirmation and accolades provided to them by white people. What often happens is that this affirmation and affection is rooted in a paternalism that is rooted in white supremacy. This paternalism is often animated by the idea that Black communities are merely pathological and that white people are needed to save Black youth from this cesspool of pathology. Many white people may not consciously believe this, but it is the framework in which their positions in these kinds of struggle are predicated. Many white liberals who engage Black issues have not ever been subjected to Black leadership and authority, particularly the kind of Black leadership that is directly from the community and deals with the particular issues of concern. These white liberals do not have the capacity to see Black people who are *of* and *from* the affected communities as leaders. This incapacity translates to the students as well. The students involved in youth advocacy in Baltimore have usually never interacted with a Black person leading these political struggles. This self-reinforcing cycle of white adult leadership and black student followers perpetuates white supremacy and Black inferiority.

There are two particular incidents that highlight the white non-profit community's inability to see Black adults as the necessary leaders of these struggles. In the summer of 2013, LBS put on a public debate about this very issue. It was a debate between me (Dayvon Love) and Zeke Cohen, the executive director of the Intersection (which is a non-profit organization that teaches young people about community organizing). It was a friendly but contentious debate about the role of white people in struggles for racial and social justice. During the debate, I made many of the same points that I made above. During the Q&A portion of the event, one of Zeke's students addressed me. She said she felt that I was being divisive by talking about the idea that white people use these issues to promote their agendas. She said that Zeke has been a big influence on her and that instead of pushing people like him away that we should be thankful for people like him who decide to come and help Black people. What she said next really struck me; she used an analogy that "Black people are like drug addicts, and that white people are like people who aren't on drugs. You cannot have someone who is on drugs trying to help someone else who is on drugs; you need someone who is clean to help people on drugs to be clean." This really struck me because not only was the analogy imperfect (people who are addicted to drugs typically *are* helped by people who are also addicted to drugs), but that her concept of Black people is of pure pathology. I asked her what are the gifts of being Black? Her response was less strong than her description of Black people as pathological. This demonstrates the way that even in progressive circles, Black youth internalize notions of Black inferiority and white supremacy.

The second incident I want to recall happened right in the midst of the Youth Jail fight. LBS had been inactive in the alliance that white-led non-profits and foundations created to fight the Youth Jail. Later, however, we made a strategic move to join the alliance. At one meeting we (LBS) suggested that the alliance declare publicly that it is a Black-led coalition. We suggested that those of us who are of and from the community be in the driver's seat for the coalition. The response to this was fascinating. No one was willing to disagree with this framing, but the level of discomfort in the room was visible. Many of the white adults nervously fumbled around the issue. You could tell that for many of the people in the room, it was the first time that they had ever been asked to question the way that their whiteness implicated their role in fighting this fight. It was rare that they had ever been in a space where a Black person asserted that we should be the leaders of any movement that primarily affects us. I often feel like I am in a unique position. During the time this fight was happening I was in my mid-20s. This made me a little too old to be seen like a youth, but young enough where I think people were more willing to hear what I have to say because youth tends to be perceived in this context as less threatening. Many of my mentors have said that they have made the point of Black leadership in similar contexts with white liberals and it becomes a point of fierce contention. I often wondered why I didn't get the same push back, and I am assuming my age has something to do with it. Ultimately our call for this alliance to be framed as a Black led effort was accepted, but only in jest. The principle of an alliance guided by Black leadership requires so much re-education and organizational restructuring that in retrospect was not a feasible demand of that group. I think that pushing that as a part of the conversation was important, but the people in this kind of alliance are limited in their ability to actually live up to what effective white-ally ship looks like in a meaningful way.

Ultimately, toward the end of the Youth Jail fight, the Maryland Department of Correction and the Department of Juvenile Services convened a meeting with the non-profit entities and foundations in the alliance to strike a deal to stop the jail. LBS was not invited to attend this meeting. This again demonstrates the way in which Black grassroots leadership is disregarded. Those of us on the front line of the fight are not seen as worthy negotiators on these issues that most directly affect us. This fundamental contradiction explains the way in which white supremacy informs the inability of people to see Black people as having the collective wherewithal to manage and operate large institutions. Until this mythology is dispelled we will be subject white to control over the institutions that train people to do youth advocacy.

Non-profit industrial complex

LBS wrote an article for our website criticizing Hathaway Ferebee as an exemplar of the *Non-Profit Industrial Complex*. The article referred to a rally that her organization "Safe and Sound" held in downtown Baltimore to fight the Youth Jail. Our general criticism was that she was front and center at the event in such a way that represented her as the leader of the movement against the youth jail. There was not an explicit acknowledgement of the Black grassroots organizations that were involved in this struggle. This perpetuates the dynamic of white people using our issues to create organizations and generate resources in ways that crowd out authentic Black leadership. I want to use this section to make it clear that this critique is not exclusive to Hathaway Ferebee. In fact, our use of the rally and her organization as an example has caused people to reduce our critique to an interpersonal beef, as opposed to an observation about the political implications of the work of white led non-profit organizations. We don't have any personal animus toward Ferebee. Instead, we detest the structure that produced her and people like her.

People attempted to reduce our critique to sentimental and emotional critique, as oppose to a substantive critique. There was a radio program that aired during the youth jail fight that addressed this issue of the role of the non-profit industrial complex. It was a show that included two state delegates, Rev. Heber Brown, and other youth involved in the Youth Jail fight. There was a moment where I made the point about their being an industry where people profiteer off of the misery of Black people. The push back from this was quite interesting. Del. Heather Mizuer said that she knows Hathaway Ferebee and that my statement seemed to suggest negative things about Ferebee's character that she did not like. She made it a point to say that we all have the same goal in emphasizing her support of Hathaway. The tone of her response was one of great concern over the implications of this criticism. This is typically what happens in these conversations. A substantive critique of how Black people's issues are used to prop up other people's organizations gets re-directed to a conversation about not tarnishing the character of an individual white person. I also want to point out that we do not have the same goal. This is often used to obscure necessary scrutiny of those who are engaged in these political struggles. My goal is to build independent Black power in our communities. Fighting the Youth Jail for LBS is a part of that goal. People like Mizeur and Ferebee have never demonstrated a desire to support and give deference to independent Black institutions. They are in positions to use our issues to promote a "progressive" political agenda that has as its end game to fortify white liberal organizations and their political power. Again, this is not a critique exclusively of Ferebee, in fact there are many other organization and individuals that fit this critique more than she does, but in the context of the Youth Jail fight it was important for us to demonstrate what it looks like in practice when white folks usurp the social capital from work on these issues to fortify their own organizations.

People here have a hard time understanding our critique outside of the context of an interpersonal squabble, however. WYPR, in a series called "The Line Between US," did a segment on this concept of the non-profit industrial complex. It began with me reading an essay that I wrote about the youth jail and the problem of white co-option. What struck me most about this segment was Sheila Kast's inability to articulate the position that I put forward in my essay. Her challenge to the idea I put forth was that the framework of Black led institutions leading the way on this issues doesn't make sense in a state that is majority white. She said "how can you exercise Black control on the issue of the Youth Jail if most of the elected officials making decisions about it are white?" This comment really perplexed me. Obviously Black control doesn't mean that Black people control the state government. Black control means control of the institutions that directly represent and serve the interest of Black people. Black control means being the executive directors of the organizations that create the public policy agenda that the white legislators vote on.

One of the biggest impediments to understanding the substance of this critique is that people tend to moralize issues of justice: people tend to talk about the people who are involved as having a moral imperative to get involved. This lens obscures the role of self-interest. I would argue that self- interest had more to do with why these non-profit organizations got involved than a moral imperative to help Black youth. Many of the non-profit organizations that worked on the Youth Jail issue had contracts with the Department of Corrections to do programming with incarcerated youth. Their concern about challenging the youth jail coincided with a move to cut their funding to do programming inside of prison. These organizations stood to benefit financially if money could be taken from the construction of a jail and put into "youth programs." Much of the money that would be gained would go right into the pockets of the white executive leadership, and those of us who are of and from the community would only get the crumbs.

Another example of the non-profit industrial complex operating during the Youth Jail fight was a planned celebration for stopping the construction of the Youth Jail. We are a part of an informal group of Black leaders called the Better Maryland Committee (BMC). Many of the other members of this small group are Black elders who helped us fight against the Youth Jail. There were members of this group who have had bad experiences with the organizations that were a part of the white-led Youth Jail alliance that we had strategically joined. The experience of white people exploiting Black children and profiting off of it left a bad taste in the mouth of many of the well-respected elders in this group. Many of these experiences preceded the arrival of the current alliance members. I deliberately chose not to call a meeting where these two groups were present, however, because I knew this would still lead to conflict. After the announcement of the halt of the Youth Jail, this alliance planned a celebration at an independent college in Baltimore called Sojourner-Douglass College. Incidentally, this is the place where the BMC regularly convened, and the celebration was slated to happen the same night as a BMC meeting. We weren't even aware that this celebration was happening. One of our executive board members had given out information about one of our contacts at Sojourner-Douglass College without asking for details. This oversight is what allowed this celebration to get planned there. The day before the event was scheduled to happen, we were visited by some mentors of ours, Heber Brown and Chabria Thomas. They asked us about this event at Sojourner Douglass. Functionally they told us that we needed to find a way to stop it. We understood the implications of this celebration happening while the BMC was meeting. We immediately called the appropriate people at the college to have the event cancelled. I then made a phone call to the some of the youth leaders and the non-profit folks who were putting this event on. Needless to say they were very upset with me. I explained to them the problem as much as I could without giving away too much confidential information.

In the midst of making these phone calls I had a very interesting conversation with a youth (but older youth) who was a part of one of the non-profit organizations organizing the celebration. He said that based on our conversations about the non-profit industrial complex and comments that had been made by Rev Brown that he felt that we were saying that he was being mindlessly manipulated by white people. I explained to him that our point wasn't that he didn't have a mind of his own, but that all of his work was providing social and human capital to organizations with a history of exploiting Black people. I tried to explain to him that in spite of his good work and intentions these organizations are not ultimately accountable to Black people, but to white philanthropy that uses our issues to prop up their institutions. I could tell that he was still troubled. He wasn't really able to hear the point that I was making, which was that his presence as a specifically Black youth gave the organization legitimacy that allowed them to put money in the pockets of people with no material or existential stake in the livelihood of Black people. Here you can see another problem with the intervention of white liberals into the Black community. People generally don't like to be told that they are being used by others. It creates the impression that they don't have their own minds. This makes it difficult to tell young people about the dynamic of the non-profit industrial complex. It creates situations like this where I have to be very delicate about how I explain the argument I'm making about non-profits to avoid creating unnecessary conflict between people who need to be unified in order to effectively fight on these issues.

Some people might have been rattled for having to cancel an event like this. There was a lot of anger toward me for months. But I didn't care. As someone committed to Pan-Afrikan Nationalism, I only care about what will get us closer to that objective. Anything short of that is not on my agenda. Some of the young people in the alliance were upset because they really wanted a celebration.

Unfortunately a lot of our youth have never experience any kind of political victory. It provided a huge boost in self-esteem for people to say that they were a part of an effort stop the youth jail. What is more important to me is that we properly organize to have a sustainable strategy for our liberation. Even though this celebration would have been nice, to have these two groups in the same place would have undermined our credibility with the very people who have the expertise we need to be successful. Put a little more bluntly, I can afford to be in bad favor with the people caught up in the non-profit industrial complex. They are not the people who matter: the people who matter are the people in our communities who have been struggling to fight these issues before a lot of these non-profits even existed.

Community Organizing

There are a lot of organizations that say they work with the "community." The term *community* is an abstraction that people have come to use to stand in for the objects of the political battles that people are waging. This happens similarly with the term *youth*. People throw these terms around, but typically the people who are being talked about are merely just used to support a particular political agenda. During the Youth Jail fight there was a lot of talk about community organizing, but there was a very piecemeal and limited strategy that was deployed. One strategy that the Youth Jail alliance used that demonstrates a limited view on organizing was their sponsorship of "community meetings." They would organize such meetings at places in the community to talk about the Youth Jail.

If you know anything about the communities in Baltimore, you know that there are already a lot of meetings that go on: community association meetings, after-school programs, etc. The best way to get the community involved in an effort is to attend meetings that are already going on and ask to speak. The key is to start with people who are already involved in their communities. This oversight by the non-profit organizations attempting to organize on these issues is caused by their notion that there aren't people in the community already attempting to organize. Often the idea is that they need to *create* a sensibility against issues that harm our communities. People in our communities have already been working on important issues. The problem is that we typically don't have access to the kinds of resources that white liberals get access to. People like Kimberly Armstrong, who is a long time advocate in Baltimore on youth issues, are not privy to the same kind of resources that Safe and Sound, Just Kids Partnership, the Intersection, or other white led non-profit organizations have access to. In the midst of this we are still organizing and having to use our networks to get work done. We often have to compete against white liberals for legitimacy in this arena, and we are typically crowded out. Our Black legislators are so used to seeing the white liberal advocates that when they see us they don't give us the same level of reverence. This is in part due to the notions of Black inferiority mentioned in the last section, but also to the fact that these non-profit organizations have access to the resources that give them access to more data and more professional looking materials. They are thus more likely to be taken seriously by their non-Black legislative colleagues. These non-profit organizations, whether intentionally or not, literally suck the social capital from Black people and elevate themselves to be leaders on these issues.

LBS organized during this effort differently than some of our peers in the Youth Jail Alliance. We tapped into the networks that we had developed over a few years to help bring attention to this issue. We didn't attempt to do a series of events, or try to create a new organization, but instead, understood that there are already people doing work and we need to try to bring together people who could lend us support in fighting the jail. One of the things that I did was to become a teacher. This was an intentional effort to politicize young people. I taught African American Studies and Social Justice. I used my classroom as a way to get students engaged in the fight against the Youth Jail. In fact, I took my students on several field trips to Annapolis to see how the process works. I was even able to get one of my students to testify in support of one of the bills proposed to fight the youth jail. I really miss being a teacher because it is the place where you can really see young people grow. The young people I mentored will grow up to become leaders on issues of Black Liberation in their own lives and careers.

Our organizing efforts were set apart from the work of our non-profit peers because we focused on the strategy of strengthening the networks that already exist, instead of trying to create a new network to work on the Youth Jail. This strategy was both highly effective and truly respectful of Black leaders, community members, and organizations. I don't want to give the impression that if you are in non-profit organization that we are calling you a sellout. There are individuals in these non-profit organizations and foundations who were very helpful to us. These people realized the limitation of the position that they are in, but were instrumental in giving us information that we needed to help us effectively talk to legislators. This is the proper role of people in non-profits: to be willing to provide support and resources to those of us in the grassroots. This is fundamentally different from what most non-profit organizations are used to. Usually they are setting the agenda and are being supported by the community. This is backwards. We need to be the ones guiding the strategy. Our work on the youth jail was the first step toward changing the paradigm for how we fight social justice issues in Baltimore.

Lobbying Legislators:

Legislators in cities like Baltimore are motivated by pressure. Plain and simple. Organized, constant and strong pressure. Sometimes we let the idea that politics is governed by big moneyed interest keep us from understanding what organized pressure can do to effect political outcomes. In Annapolis (Maryland's state capital) legislators from Baltimore are used to hearing more from interest groups than from the people of Baltimore. I don't say this to cast dispersion of the people of Baltimore. Many of the people in our community that are effected by the forces of poverty, and institutional racism do not have the resources and time to focus on public policy advocacy in Annapolis. They are busy trying to keep their communities together with the limited resources at their disposal. This has the effect of having legislators in Annapolis who are making decisions, knowing that they will not be called out for it. We simply don't have the public policy infrastructure that other groups have in order to represent our interest effectively.

Black legislators are often given a bad rap in discussions about why cities like Baltimore are in the condition that they are in. Don't get me wrong, there are certainly Black elite who have a willful disregard for the masses of Black people. But there are legislators that genuinly are interested in doing the bidding of the community, but get lumped in with the other legislators selling us out. Black legislators deal with paternalism from their white counterparts that creates a tremendous amount of angst. They are often disrespected and disregarded because they do not have the army of constituents and interest groups that their white counterparts have. What often happens to these legislators is that when they are elected they are sent to places like Annapolis, without a public policy infrastructure to back them up. They are usually isolated, and don't often see their constituents in the numbers they need in order to help them do the work they need to do to fight for us. I remember during the fight against the Youth Jail during a hearing in Annapolis several Black legislators being visibly inspired and motivated by the presence of young people. A vice chair of one of the committees dealing with the Youth Jail issue (who is a Black legislator) made it a point during the hearing to acknowledge the presence of the young people in the room, and was forceful at questioning the state about the necessity of a Youth Jail. As organizers it is important that we don't waste our time with legislators that are playing games, but it is also really important that we don't discount our Black elected officials outright. Many of them need us to help them help us.

One of the most important things that communities under assault need is a grassroots, community based public policy infrastructure. What often happens is that non-profits decide that they will be the public policy entity for the community. This leads to non-profit industrial complex to descend onto these communities and speak for people in communities, instead of standing behind and speaking with people in the community. The role of community organizers who are not from the communities being assailed by things like mass-incarceration and institutional racism is to help provide resources for communities to build their own public policy infrastructure. What often happens is that the notion of Black inferiority is so deep that many of the people from non-profits, who purport to want to help, can't imagine a world where they are being led by the people of the community. They often can't help but look at people in the community as children. This leads them to think that they have to be public policy infrastructure and that we follow their lead. This reproduces the problem of the non-profit industrial complex.

During the Youth Jail fight we had to simultaneously build an informal public policy infrastructure while fighting the jail. This is often the kind of flexibility that grassroots organizations are forced to develop because of the lack of access to adequate resources. We built this public policy infrastructure through developing relationships with Black led organizations including the local NAACP, Associated Black Charities, Sojourner Douglass College, the Institute of Urban Research at Morgan State University, the Legislative Black Caucus of Maryland, the local Urban League and many other organizations. The key to this networking was our ability to develop relationships with our Black elders who could help us to produce the help we needed to piece together a functional public policy infrastructure. The non-profit industrial complex inability to effectively network with these organizations demonstrates the limitations of that kind of organizing during the Youth Jail fight, and why radical Black grassroots organization are necessary to fight on these issues.

Passing Christopher's Law
By Dayvon Love

Christopher's Law and our efforts around this were much different than the fight against the youth jail. This effort was truly a grassroots effort and it represents much of what community organizing should be about. There was no foundation money, no white non-profit people, and no white liberal paternalism. This effort was collaboration between LBS, the local NAACP, the mother of Christopher Brown and her family and friends.

Christopher Brown was a young man who was killed in 2012 by an off duty police officer in Baltimore County. Christopher's death came at the heels of the Trayvon Martin incident. Delegate Jill P. Carter decided to work with Chris Brown (Christopher's mom) and her family during the 2013 legislative session to pass a law that would do two primary things. First, it would require annual and entrance training for "cultural sensitivity." This was included for the explicit purpose of getting law enforcement officers to develop race literacy and to highlight the ways in which policing has been rooted in anti-black violence. The second thing the law would do is require law enforcement officers to be able to administer CPR. This was important because the off duty officer that choked Christopher to death could have saved the young man's life if he knew CPR. This law passed the House of Delegates in 2013 but did not pass the Senate. After the session was over Delegate Carter asked LBS if we would get involved in helping to push the law through the general assembly in 2014. We accepted, and began our involvement in trying to pass Christopher's law.

It is an honor for me to have worked with Chris Brown and her family. It's really hard to fathom the courage it takes to take the lead on an issue that hits so close to home. Right away this fight did not feel like we were fighting for a cause. This did not feel like an issue in the way that something like environmental justice or animal rights is often represented in political discussions. This felt like we were fighting to protect our mothers and our brothers. Chris Brown's pain was not an abstraction, or merely a political position, it was the body of a mother responding to the white supremacist society that produced the devaluation of her son and many of us Black men and boys. No one was trying to get a grant to do programming. No one was trying to advance their political careers. This was a controversial issue that went to the heart of a core problem of our society, the disregard for the fundamental humanity of Black people.

Several meetings took place over the summer and fall before the legislative session began. In Maryland the legislative session is 90 days and begins in January. People who are serious about getting things passed through the Maryland general assembly must take the time during the months before the session starts to plan and strategize. The legislative session is so tightly packed that it is rare for an issue that comes up fresh during the session to become law.

Most successful legislative strategies come to Annapolis with bills that are already done. In our planning meetings we talked about a media strategy, which legislators we ought to focus on speaking with, and how to bring the community out to Annapolis. We were very busy all the way up until the beginning of the legislative session.

In October of 2013 a forum was held at Morgan State University to address issues of police/community relations. It was convened by the Legislative Black Caucus of Maryland, chaired by Delegate Aisha Braveboy from Prince George's County. Delegates Jill P. Carter and Cheryl Glenn were present along with Senator Joan Carter Conway. This was very significant because here you had four Black women legislators taking the lead on an issue that plagues Black people. You also had the Baltimore Police Commissioner, the Sheriff, and other law enforcement personnel present. This added to the significance of the event because it was a Black organization, led by Black people, holding public officials accountable on an issue that faces our people every day. It is not often that our public officials are beholden to Black organizations. We usually find that liberal white organizations like the ALCU or other non-profit organizations take the lead on these kinds of issues when you have such high level public officials present. Justin Fenton, the crime reporter for the Baltimore Sun was even present for part of the evening. The forum took place a few months after a gentleman named Tyrone West was killed in the custody of Morgan State police. This sparked a lot of outrage amongst the family and many people who were in the community. When I showed up the room was packed. Chris Brown was there, and there were many other families there. The forum was set up to allow the community to air the grievances against the law enforcement. It began as a simple panel discussion and then opened for Q&A. I asked the first the question. I asked if law enforcement in Baltimore is ready to talk about institutional racism and go beyond the general notion of bias that most people refer to when they are talking about racism. The Commissioner responded with an answer that basically fed into the criticism I was making about the superficial way in which people think about racism. He said that his agency has a program in place designed to deal with all bias, not just racial bias and that this measure was an example of his department going well beyond the call of duty to deal not only with racism but other forms of bias and bigotry. This response is the classic form of liberalism that crowds out structural analysis of racism. The move of not focusing on institutional racism assumes that the problem is rooting out bigoted police officers, instead of understanding the internalized notions of anti-blackness that are inherent in American society. This misunderstanding is something that would become a common theme throughout the fight to pass Christopher's Law.

After I asked my question something happened that I will remember for the rest of my life. Family after family came up and talked about the deaths of their loved ones at the hands of the police. I'm not talking about 3 or 4, I mean family after family had heart wrenching stories about police brutality and the disregard that law enforcement had for the pain of their families. One woman came up to the mic with her granddaughter and explained how her teenage daughter was struck by a speeding police car and killed. She said that police department didn't even respond to her until 180 days after the incident, and the response was just an acknowledgment that there needed to be an investigation. The pain in the room was so thick that I could feel it in my lungs.

I thought that this would be in the Baltimore Sun for sure. Here you have Justin Fenton who is a well respected journalist for a major paper covering a major event. You have a Black led organization, with four Black women legislators convening a forum where Black people, who typically don't get a chance to have their pain heard in public, are able to levy complaints to the Commissioner of Baltimore City Police. Unfortunately, there was not a story in the Sun about this forum. This demonstrated again to me the existence of institutional racism in the Baltimore Sun and most mainstream news media in Baltimore. Black death is constantly represented in mainstream media in Baltimore. Black violence is rendered hyper visible in local new media as well. I don't think I have to do any work here to substantiate this claim; there is so much of it that to deny this would be an act of immense willful denial.

With this in mind you would think that an event where Black people are showing the institutional fortitude to address issues of institutional racism would be an important story to make the public aware of. This disrupts the dominant narrative around Black death and violence. I don't know the specifics of the logistics around news agencies and how they cover stories. But what I do know is that the lack of representations of Black capacity and of positive representations of Black life has the effect of perpetuating the invisibility of Black suffering and a belief in notions of Black inferiority. If most of the images we see in news media of Black people are violence, death and pathology then this produces a subliminal message that this is all that Black people are capable of. This is even more reason why the forum would have been a great story to make the public aware of, in order to challenge these ideas that are so prevalent in this white supremacist society. What was even worse is that after the forum Delegate Carter received a phone call from a representative of the police department where she was told that she set the Commissioner up. She was told that they were offended that their officers were referred to as murderers and that she should have stopped it. This demonstrates so much disregard for Black life. Instead of a response rooted in remorse and interest in addressing the pain of the people who were present, the Police Department was more concerned about being perceived as "murderers." What is even more problematic is that this response, to many people, is completely legitimate. There are many people who are unwilling to see the death of Black people at the hands of law enforcement as a crime. The prevalence of violence against Black people by the police is only tolerated because of the disregard for Black life. If white women were being killed once every 28 hours due to police brutality, there would certainly be a public outcry calling for a complete reformation of their practices. This forum helped to remind me why Christopher's Law is so important. We need to get law enforcement and the general public past the simple discourse of bigotry and bias, and to a more sophisticated understanding of institutional racism that is embedded in the collective consciousness of Americans.

Leading up to the legislative session we appeared on various radio shows to raise awareness about the Christopher's Law. What had been added to the 2014 bill was a requirement to have law enforcement officers trained to deal with people who have developmental disabilities. Robert Saylor was killed in police custody in 2013. He was a young man with a developmental disability. This sparked huge outrage and advocates for people with disabilities reached out to Delegate Carter and asked her to include this in Christopher's Law. Adding this to the law changed tremendously the way that the bill was received. On the Marc Steiner Show in Baltimore we had one segment where those of us in support of the bill came speak on it. The segment included Delegate Jill Carter, Delegate Michael Smigel, Byron Warnken and Chris Brown joined us later. What I noticed about this conversation was that there was a level of sympathy and empathy extended to the issues of disabled people being protected from violence, that didn't not seemed to be extended to the issue of Black people being abused and killed. The callers and the other guest seemed more comfortable talking about the injustice of all people who are abused by police, instead of the historic and systemic problem of Black people being targets of police brutality. One way to look at this is that the inclusion of the protection against those who are disabled liberalized the bill in order for people who otherwise are indifferent to Black suffering to have a reason to support the bill. I am not making this observation as a way to discount and discredit the importance of protecting people with disabilities, but to demonstrate that in civil society that there is more willingness to acknowledge the oppression of those with disabilities than those who will acknowledge the humanity of Black people.

Organizing for this campaign was a lot easier because we had an established base of students that we had developed relationships over the years. The youth jail fight gave us a base that was already mobilized and trusted us. The young people I'd taught when I was a teacher still maintained interest in supporting these kinds of efforts. My primary organizing work during this campaign was to bring young people to Annapolis on hearing day to show that there are youth effected by the law who were willing to stand up and be heard. I also was able to reach out to others who were interested in showing their support. Chris Brown had organized her friends, family and other mothers whose sons had been killed by the police. This was probably the strongest force during the fight to pass Christopher's Law. They guided the agenda and the way that this fight was carried out - organizations like LBS and the local NAACP provided the support needed to push this effort through.

During the House judiciary committee hearing many interesting dynamics played themselves out. We brought young people down from Baltimore on the Pleasant Hope Baptist Church Bus. Pleasant Hope has always been supportive of our work. Many people's perception of youth is that they are not interested in how government works. But these youth had some very strong reactions to the hearing that I will return to later.

During the actual testimony on the first panel there was a very contentious exchange. The first panel included Delegate Jill Carter, Tessa Hill-Alston who is president of Baltimore Chapter of the NAACP, Chris Brown, and a gentleman representing the disabled community whose named I can't recall. As Delegate Carter mentioned the need for law enforcement to change in order to address its issues with the community, Delegate McDermott accused Delegate Carter of blaming law enforcement for the violence in Baltimore city. He was very impassioned in his challenge to what he perceived as Delegate Carter denigrating the honorable service of law enforcement officers. As she clarified that her point was that law enforcement needs to take responsibility for the impacts that their practices have on Black people. Before the back and forth could go much further the chairman of the committee angrily dismissed this panel and asked for the next panel to come up. This demonstrates how the emotional baggage that is projected onto issues of race forms a barrier to addressing the concerns of people who are targets of racism. Delegate McDermott did what many white people do when Black people make institutional demands to address racism, which is to blame us for being mean, or insensitive and take the focus away from the pain and suffering that Black people continue to face at the hands of law enforcement.

The subsequent panels were less eventful, and many others testified. Law enforcement testified against the bill. They made the claim that there was no need to legislate law enforcement to address these issues because it was already a part of their training. It was troubling that their testimony continued to forward a conceptual understanding of racism that was based in the liberal discourse of bias and bigotry, instead of the more sophisticated and structural aspects of racism that make it so insidious. The reaction from the students was priceless. They were really mad at the chairman of the committee and at Delegate McDermott. To them, what Delegate Carter said was completely clear and very diplomatic. The level of emotion involved in the behavior of the chair and the delegate was seen by the students as completely irrational. It made them so mad that people would treat this issue with such hostility. I think this was an important experience for the students because a lot of times when they hear people talk about racism and white people's resistance to acknowledging its existence, they don't get to see it play out in politics first hand. But the hearings allowed them to see how institutional racism actually operates in the structures of government.

Christopher's Law was eventually passed. The combination of our social media campaigning, student organizing, Chris Brown organizing mothers and the indispensability of Delegate Jill Carter we were able to get this bill passed. This was completely a grassroots effort that demonstrates the power of what we can do without the intervention of white led and controlled organizations attempting to use our issues as causes for their own political purposes.

Conclusion: On Interracial Coalitions and Next Steps
By Lawrence Grandpre

This project aimed to have those us at LBS to address the numerous ways dominant intellectual frameworks for academic study and political action have limited necessary attempts to advance social justice from black perspectives. As we have advocated for social justice conversations and political actions to address white supremacy/anti-blackness as central concerns, the incorporation of African centered thought and the importance of independent black institutions, we faced many concerns and objections to our framework. While it is beyond the scope of this initial volume to thoroughly address all of these issues, we thought it necessary to address one specific concern: the so called "Black-White Binary." The concern here is that focusing on black experiences and black oppression limits the discussion around racism so that it centers on Black oppression and in the process obscures the reality of the oppression of other racial groups, specifically Latinos and Asians. While the earlier piece on anti-blackness helps to contextualize the continued reality of anti-black racism and details some of the mechanics of oppression that are specific to Blacks in America, many advocates of inter-racial coalitions still argue that our framing is "divisive" and hurts the possibility of producing effective multiracial coalitions. This chapter serves as an opportunity to recap some of issues we have discussed and apply them to the specific problem of interracial coalitions. We hope that readers can take from this a set of lessons to guide their next steps.

The argument about Black scholarship hurting interracial coalitions ignores the reality that Blacks do not choose to adopt Black-White binary thinking in order to give themselves privileged status in discussion of anti-racism. Instead, we have been historically forced into power relations that functioned to produce a white over black political/historical reality. Professors Katerina Deliovsky and Tamari Kitossa explain that historically, European and American whites have used black skin as a mirror in which whites reflected upon themselves as virtuous and superior. To properly understand racism one must recognize the historical truth behind this "Black/white Mancianism" (a term they borrowed from Frantz Fanon). Within this phenomenon are certain experiences which are unique to Blacks in America. While other groups had ethnic enclaves that reflected cultural continuity with a homeland that contextualized their struggles against racism, blacks had a violent middle passage. This experience separated them from the essential cultural resources of their homeland and found their attempts at ethnic/cultural healing violently suppressed both on the plantation (forced separation of Black families, destruction of indigenous languages and religious systems) and after (the bombing of black wall street; Jim Crow segregation and the denial of essential basic services; forced migration via lynchings and economic bias in the South which further strained family/ cultural ties; housing bias and white flight once black communities got a foothold in major cities; COINTELPRO targeting and the destruction of the MOVE organization which featured the violent destruction Black communal empowerment efforts). This history reflects the reality of whiteness affirming itself through the negrophilia/ negrophobia paradox that is unique to Blacks in America. For example, while Mexicans were lynched in the southwest, they could often flee to Mexico, while blacks lack a homeland that provides them protection. Also, as professors Roy Brooks and Kristen Wilder note, the numbers of lynchings of Blacks represent a pattern of systemic terror for Blacks as distinct from a specific law enforcement strategy for Mexicans. Finally, Cornel West, among others, notes that it was unique for whites to castrate and sexually mutilate Blacks in lynchings, showing how not mere "racism" but a specific notion of communal (white) affiliation and psycho/sexual affirmation was present with the black lynched body. All of these factors make the Black experience unique. If Blacks are to properly understand their position in America, they must confront the reality that the world has specific ways of relating to them. We must learn our specific history because contemporary inequity and injustice stem from this specific experience.

The need for Blacks to study their own social location is essential not only to combat individual policies that target them, but also to develop independent institutions to protect their collective interests. Naim Akbar described how conditions on the plantation breed a hatred of work and the tendency of using work stoppages and slowdowns as a form of self preservation and resistance. The contemporary manifestations of this historical trauma reflect in the tendency for many Blacks to enter underground economies rather than take jobs where their work would serve the interests of dominant powers, many of whom benefited historically from slavery. Seeing the Black economic situation as related to a plantation experience is essential. It shows that a key part of the struggle for Black communal empowerment is to address the unique psychic scars the Black community suffered in slavery. This is a precondition for advocating progressive independent black institutions that can give Black people a critical sense of ownership in their work and thereby help to break the psychological chains of slavery. With ownership, the creativity and drive of those whose desire the freedom that only an underground existence can give now might be harnessed can benefit the community might otherwise drive them toward the underground economy, often in activities that hurt the community, into a resource for communal empowerment. In conversations with other people of color, we've heard a focus on independent black institutions be called anti-coalitions or even reverse racism, a claim which ignores the unique history of anti-black racism and the necessity of independent black institutions to counter this history. To paraphrase Malcolm X, we didn't land on the Black/white binary; the Black/white binary landed on us, it is only through engaging the reality of White over Black oppression in America that Blacks as a community can begin to collectively advance.

Seen in this light, it is strange that it has become more or less accepted scholarly practice over the past few decades to critique and avoid the "Black/white binary". Far from denying that other oppressions exist, this binary is simply a tool to help evaluate, understand and frame the forms of oppression in the world. It is a tool that gives unique (but admittedly not comprehensive) insights into how power works. Part of the reason this frame of analysis has been so vociferously critiqued is the same white (academic) liberal anti-blackness discussed in the previous chapters. Moreover, when the Black/white paradigm (specifically the notion of anti-blackness as a global system) is applied to relations between Latinos/Asians and Blacks, the unfortunate reality of anti-blackness without other non-white cultures becomes apparent. Latin America has a long history of colorism and discrimination against descendants of African slaves, from the forced removal of Blacks from Argentina in the late 19th century, to violence against Black Haitians in contemporary Dominican Republic and the hypersexualization of Black women throughout Brazilian history. The famous Mexican "mestizaje" (or mixture) theorist Vasconcelos argued that Mexicans could become a "cosmic race" via their mixed white (Spanish) and brown (indigenous) bloodlines (and in the process, breed out undesirable black bloodlines). Moreover, the legacy of Arab enslavement of Africans (including the production of eunuchs and female servants for Arab families in the 11th and 12th centuries), the circulation of racist caricatures of Blacks in contemporary Japanese culture and, as Dutch historian Frank Dikotter notes in his book *The Discourse of Race in Modern China*, the long history (pre-dating European colonization) of China associating nobility and purity with white skin and consequentiality associating barbarism, violence and poverty with Black skin, shows anti-blackness to be a truly global phenomenon.

This is not to say all Asian and Latino/a individuals harbor anti-black sentiments (our discussion of the negrophilia/negrophobia paradox shows we hold a more nuanced conception of how anti-blackness operates), but the reality is that this fundamentally complicates notions of "POC coalitions", for, as Wilderson states, it is possible for other people of color to be against white supremacy and still be anti-black. For example, many Asian/Latino political demands as immigrants (such as the DREAM act) are often framed as seeking access to the benefits of the society, and by using the Black slave experience as a lens for evaluation these political demands are revealed to be for "democratic" dispersal of the benefits of America that have accrued through years of slavery, proving Wilderson's argument. In contrast, the Black radical tradition calls for a fundamental renegotiation of the terms of American society (through policies such as reparations) or the rejection of the call for integration into the system of white supremacy (through autonomous institution building). In this vein, the Black/white binary is revealed to be a specific, but not exclusionary tool. Other people of color can modify it to fit their own needs in evaluating and strengthening their own politics. Asian Americans theorists can and have used some Black scholarship to deconstruct how the myth of the Asian "model minority" is used to eschew discussion of Asian poverty and to blame Blacks for their own poverty. Latino/a theorists have used some examples from Black scholarship to critique the nationalist/militaristic notions of the "citizenship" advocates (such as those who advocate military service as a potential path for American citizenship). Just as the academic Black studies movement of the 1960s helped spur movements for Chicano/a, LGBT, and Native American studies, so can contemporary applications Black/white binary and the call for independent institutions be taken up by other peoples to extend the discussion of racial justice for all.

Far from being self centered or anti-coalition, our arguments reflect the reality that it is only when Black people have worked through the historical and contemporary realities of white supremacy and have developed a framework for communal empowerment that effective coalitional work can begin and the issues presented by theorists critiquing the "Black/white Binary" can be addressed. Juan Perea, one of the first theorists to gain notoriety for an academic critique of the "Black/white binary", framed his argument around the potential for legal theories and public discourse to not see Latino suffering in the face the conversation being monopolized by Blacks, a fear he say impacts the framing of anti-discrimination legislation in ways that potentially bias the laws toward Blacks. The reality is that those laws have failed to substantially help Latino/as in America not because they were biased in favor of Blacks, but because the very notion of a liberal legal framework for addressing racism breaks down in the face of white supremacy/anti-blackness. As previous chapters explain, given the reality of America's embedded racial logic and the abstract nature of racial logic, the ability to enforce even potentially progressive laws (like the Affordable Care Act) falls apart, and the ability to present truly radical solutions (like universal health care) is shattered by embedded racial logic. Perea's argument boils down to a misplaced belief in the legal framework and a sense of being slighted within public discourse. Depending on liberal political sentiment (such as the non-profit industrial complex) and legal remedies ultimately leave all people of color waiting for a transformative moment that is impossible within the existing framework. Better to take the more transformative path towards producing autonomous economic/ political power and therefore make such miracles of white benevolence unnecessary.

Ironically, it is only through the framework of self-determination and independence discussed in this book that we can transcend the "oppression Olympics" that come from competing for white liberal patronage through non-profit money and the tenuous promises of investment made by dysfunction political entities.   Strong, self-sufficient and self-determined communities make for stronger alliances between oppressed groups. For example, Mexican-Americans, Mexicans, and African Americans have all been disproportionately affected by a racist War on Drugs. In the status quo academics critique Black theorists for ignoring Mexican hyper-incarceration, while Black political theorists argue for the end of discriminatory mandatory minimum sentences for crack cocaine vs. powdered cocaine, with many others from different political affiliations argue for legalization/decriminalization. The political logic behind these moves is hailed as progressive, revolving around questions such as:

- Where is the empirical data to show the discriminatory impacts of the drug war?

- How do we make sure all voices are heard in these discussions?

- Are their pragmatic alliances (such as with those concerned with prison/ law enforcement costs) that we can make to advance our agenda?

- Where are the policy analysts who can do the lobbying or think tank style work to get a policy agenda passed through the government?

While these efforts are hailed as "progressive", they are fraught with limitations, pitfalls, and missed opportunities, and must be supplemented with a discussion of culture, independent institution building and a recognition of reality of white supremacy/ anti-blackness. This framework raises entirely distinct questions, such as:

- What are the cultural/economic reasons people use and sell drugs now? What resource (cultural/faith/ etc.) do our communities have to address this problem? How can they be strengthened? What can be learned from African societies which had no word for "jail" because imprisonment was unnecessary in those communities? How can communities of color build capacity to be sure that, in a world of legalization, we ensure our brothers and sisters won't use (legalized) drugs for psychological escapes from oppression?

- Given the socio-economic conditions that force people into the drug trade, could a call for lesser mandatory minimum be akin to dictating slave masters give their slave fewer lashes for plantation transgressions? Is this policy change, hailed as one of the prime success stories of race-conscious liberal politics, actually conservative in this framework?

- Does the focus on empirical data assume people would change their minds if they knew enforcement was biased? Given America's psycho-social dynamics around race, what makes us think quantitative proof of discriminatory impacts would change beliefs? Might there not even be pleasure in the idea that policing is over-focused on minority communities, given the myth of the drug crazed, irrational brown person and the pleasure people get from seeing brown bodies policed (think the T.V. show *Cops*)?

- What are the downfalls of framing the case for legalization/decriminalization around economic cost and liberal notions of colorblind legal "equality", versus a framework of redistributive racial justice and communal empowerment? Won't this liberal political logic be used against other community empowerment causes, with this cost-conscious framing justifying cutting/ privatizing social services, especially those that are targeted to poor/blacks and thus not "legally colorblind/equal access"? How might legalization tax money/ decriminalization savings to go to rich/white communities and thus actually exacerbate, not eliminate racial inequality?

- How can we get tax revenue/ savings from decriminalization to fund culturally competent prisoner rehabilitation? How do we produce economic opportunity for those in the drug trade who might lose their income if legalization were to happen? Should we condition our support for decriminalization/legalization on these sorts of stipulations?

When these questions are asked, better solutions begin to appear and only then can productive coalitions be formed. For example, given the reality of mutual harm from the American War on Drugs, it could be possible to parallel the Black call for reparations for slavery with a call for Mexican, Mexican-American, and Black reparations for the War on Drugs. Adopting UC-San Diego professor Charles Brooks' framework for reparations for slavery, federal and state investment in community development banks that give loans and grants to those who live in communities most affected by the War on Drugs could serve as a framework for this policy's implementation. Social service grants would go to cultural competency prisoner rehabilitation programs, youth criminal justice diversion programs such as urban gardens, and priority would be given to residents of the community (ironically flipping "white flight" into a mechanism to protect these funds against "white savior" non-profit cooption). Priority for business loans/ grants would be given to focus on local co-operative economic opportunity in communities that have suffered from racially biased enforcement practices. Each community would be able to use funds in ways indigenous to their own unique cultures.

Thus, the framework of independent institutions opens up new, unseen possibilities for interracial co-operation. These opportunities open up when we use the Black radical tradition as a guide and go through, not around, the Black-white paradigm of racism. Recognizing the unique experience of Blacks in America is vital for learning the lessons that will help us each, no matter our differences, live in strong and self-determined communities..

Key Reflections
By Dayvon Love

Throughout this book we have described our vision of the world and how we should approach social transformation. We want to take some time here to explicitly lay out specific action steps that we think are necessary in order to move us closer to the development of institutional capacity and independent Black power.

Reframe the narrative of our struggle:

Often the white left describes the struggle of Black people in America as being the story of a people who are broken and deficient due to the onslaught of white supremacy/anti-blackness. This situates our Blackness as a pathology that needs to be removed, instead of the extension of a legacy of people of African descent that must be supported. Typically Blackness as an identity foregrounds our experience of suffering. Instead, we must illuminate the strengths that exist in our communities as the focal point of how we narrate the Black Freedom Struggle. We are not a people who are defined by our brokenness, but a people who are defined by our ability to survive the most monstrous destruction of human life in the history of the world. The strength and brilliance that it has taken to survive and function in the system of global white supremacy/anti-blackness should be studied, built upon and narrated by us. This means that we don't need white people to save us - we need to work to build and maintain our own lives and institutions.

Focus on the development of local community power with an eye to the national mainstream:

Our issues often get swept up into a national political conversation in which we have very little actual power. Politics should start with local political power because this is the only way to effectively build a base. When we obsess over interjecting ourselves into the national political mainstream we are swept up into a discursive context that is impotent at building power in the hands of the people in our society that are the most dispossessed. We must be politically astute and have an awareness of how we relate to the larger national political context, but we must keep our feet rooted in the local community in order to build power.

Train young people:

Many organizations that fight for Black Liberation are personality driven. These organizations often revolve around a charismatic leader and tend to rely very little on its membership's substantive input. This can lead to a situation where the development of new leadership is not prioritized. When the old leader moves on, there is no one to take their place and the entire organization must be reinvented from scratch if it is to exist at all. We must train youth at every step of the process so that leadership can be passed along in order that our institutions do not live or die on the strength of just one person.

Be entrepreneurial:

The non-profit model often frames out the notion of doing business in a way that is socially responsible. While there are roles that non-profit organizations can play, we must develop business ventures that build in Black communities first financial sustainability and independence then wealth and eventually political power. Many of the big non-profits use our labor, suffering and human capital to build the social and political capital of white people who run social service organizations. These are resources that we should use to develop our own institutions. We cannot settle for charity, we must build our own power.

Do not allow people to emotionalize arguments about independent Black institutions:

People can get very uncomfortable talking about race. People are even more uncomfortable with the notion of independent Black power. Often the idea of developing power among Black people is cast as some aggressive, offensive attack against white people. Such a depiction distracts the conversation away from being about empowering Black people and towards how we can make more people feel good about being in a coalition for justice. This functionally crowds out our ability to substantively build the power we need so that we are not dependent on the good will of Black people. Do not get sucked into this. This is not an argument about hating anyone – it is a position about empowering Black people. Do not take on the responsibility for white people's feelings (or anyone else's for that matter).

Take advantage of the wisdom of Black Elders who have movement history:

There is nothing new under the Sun. Many of the dynamics at play in this struggle are just extension of things that our elders have experienced already. Young people have a tendency to think that we are discovering problems that are extremely different than what our elders have seen. This leads many of us to think that we need a brand new system of ideas to achieve Black Liberation. This cannot be further from the truth. In fact, the institutions most responsible for developing healthy, productive and brilliant young people are not colleges, non-profits or after school programs. It was our grandmothers who were the foundation of a generation that had more stable families, stronger communities and world class intellects. Of course these other institutions help, but it was the rootedness that the proverbial "Big Momma" gave us that made possible many of the leaders that we respect today.

Thank you for taking the time to engage our reflections from the Baltimore grassroots. Visit us at www.lbsbaltimore.com and stay tuned for Volume 2.